Writing and learning across the curriculum 11-16

Nancy Martin
Pat D'Arcy
Bryan Newton
Robert Parker

Schools Council Writing across the Curriculum Project
University of London Institute of Education

Ward Lock Educational for The Schools Council

ISBN 0 7062 3498 7 paperback
0 7062 3499 5 hardback

First published 1976
Reprinted 1976, 1978, 1979, 1980

Set in 11 on 13 point Monotype Imprint
by Woolaston Parker Limited, Leicester
and printed by Hollen Street Press Ltd
at Slough Berkshire
for Ward Lock Educational
116 Baker Street, London W1M 2BB
A member of the Pentos Group
Made in England

Contents

Project Team members

Nancy Martin	Director 1971–6
Peter Medway	Project Officer 1971–3
Harold Smith	Project Officer 1971–4
Pat D'Arcy	Project Officer 1973–6
Bryan Newton	Project Officer 1974–6
Robert Parker	Project Officer (part-time) 1974–5

Acknowledgments

We owe a great debt to the many teachers of all subjects who have contributed to our work by their shrewd and practical comments and by their generous sharing with us of the writing and taped talking of their pupils.

We also wish to acknowledge the part played in all the work of the Project by scholars from overseas who worked with us for long periods of time, attending our weekly planning meetings and our seminars, speaking at meetings and writing contributions for our publications: Garth Boomer from South Australia, Bill Renehan from the Australian Council of Educational Research, the late Rod Morisset from NCTE.

We want to acknowledge the enormous contribution made to our thinking and ways of working by the Project Officers who worked on the first part of the Project, Peter Medway (1971–3) and Harold Smith (1971–4), and Frances Mawer our administrative assistant (1972–5) whose editorial talents helped us so greatly.

We are grateful to our Consultative Committee for their support in general and particularly for their helpful comments and suggestions about the first draft of this book.

We would like to thank the many people at the Schools Council who, from a great variety of situations, gave us the benefit of their advice. In particular we want to thank our Liaison Officers, Ian Parry and Maurice Plaskow, for always being there when we needed them. We wish to acknowledge above all our debt to Professor James Britton, the director of the original research (The Development of Writing Abilities 11-18) whose findings our Project was set up to disseminate, and a most valued member of our Consultative Committee. His thinking and advice has informed almost all our work.

5

Finally we would particularly like to thank the following schools and colleges who provided us with examples of talk and writing:

Chapter one
Trowbridge Technical College, Wiltshire
City of Leicester College of Education
King Harold School, Waltham Abbey, Essex
Chelmsford Saturday Drama School, Essex
St Paul's School, Newry, Northern Ireland
Chelsea School, London
Witney Technical College, Oxfordshire

Chapter two
Countesthorpe College, Leicestershire
Wilton Secondary (now Middle) School, Wiltshire
Thomas Bennett Comprehensive School, Crawley
Waldersdale Boys' School, Chatham
Malmesbury Comprehensive School, Wiltshire
Knottingly High School, Yorkshire
King Harold School, Waltham Abbey, Essex
Benfield Comprehensive School, Newcastle
Sandhurst School, Kent

Chapter three
Malmesbury Comprehensive School, Wiltshire
Chilwell Comprehensive School, Nottinghamshire
Leysland High School, Leicestershire
Countesthorpe College, Leicestershire
Martin High School, Leicestershire
Wreake Valley College, Leicestershire
Chelsea School, London

7

Foreword

This book, arising out of the Schools Council Development Project on Writing across the Curriculum, began as a book about writing. But by the nature of things – that is to say by the nature of language and the way it functions – it could not end there, and the book has a great deal to say about talking and reading and thinking and *learning* as these processes take place in school. Traditionally, writing has played a key role in education at the secondary level. 'Whether for reasons of economy or effectiveness,' to quote Olson and Bruner, 'schools have settled upon learning out of context through media which are primarily symbolic', and the higher up the school system we look, the more likely we are to find that the particular symbolic medium in use is that of writing. Some of the implications of the chapters that follow here constitute a challenge to this tradition, at least in so far as to suggest that it is only when school writing becomes an integral part of ongoing observing, experimenting, experiencing, talking, reading and thinking that it can fulfil its own particular learning function to the full. (To take a focal example of current misconceptions, if we cannot understand how children may learn from talking and writing we are probably *mis*interpreting the way they learn from listening and reading.)

Would it be fair to claim that secondary school teachers today have increasingly to face the task of 'educating the unwilling'? This is never the whole story, of course, in any school: every teacher knows from experience the shared pleasure of working with individual students who *want* to write what we have asked them to write, who *want* to learn what we are there to teach them. The problem is to tap the resources that go with willingness in *every* child, and it is here that pious injunctions from idealists are at their most infuriating because they so often speak as though recognising the value of such a situation were enough to bring it into being. To be fair to them, it *is* a step in the right direction to recognize that the most efficient way of getting children to learn is to get them to *want* to learn and, of course, a good deal of positively bad teaching would disappear overnight if the fact were universally recognized; but it is the steps that follow the first one that present all the problems. How can willingness and co-operation be made contagious? Sociologists and linguists who have begun to study the forces that operate against the school and against co-operative learning show how intricate and powerful a network they may sometimes form and how elaborate and far-reaching any countermeasures will have to be.

This book is concerned with what we as teachers can contribute to a solution. The writers have worked a great deal with teachers in their own schools and draw heavily upon the experience and wisdom of those teachers in presenting their story. The book does not therefore stop short at pious injunctions.

The theme of the book is not 'the teaching of English' but the role of language in learning in all parts of the curriculum. Thus, I believe it is a very timely publication: one of the most far-reaching changes in education envisaged by the Bullock Committee is to be found in its recommendation that all teachers should seek to foster learning in their particular areas by taking responsibility for the language development of their students in that area. While the Committee is no longer in existence to give or withhold its blessing, I would for my part welcome the work of the Development Project in general, and the resources of this book in particular, as noteworthy instruments in implementing that recommendation. I regard it as an honour to have been invited to associate myself with their work.

James Britton
September 1975

Reference

OLSON, D.R. and BRUNER, J.S. (1974) 'Learning through experience and learning through media' in D.R. Olson (ed) *Media and Symbols: The Forms of Expression, Communication and Education* (NSSE 73rd Yearbook Part 1) Chicago: University of Chicago Press

Introduction

The Schools Council's Writing across the Curriculum Project was set up in 1971 but its antecedents go back at least to 1966 when a research paper on *Multiple Marking of English Compositions* was published. In the course of their work for this paper, James Britton, Nancy Martin and Harold Rosen became aware of the way the writer's expectations, both of the task and of the reader, affected how he wrote – and also how the different tasks (in this case a choice of English 0 level compositions) demanded very different language operations.

In 1966 a research project was set up by the Schools Council at the London Institute of Education to look at The Written Language of 11-18 Year Olds. Its findings are summarised in chapter one of this book and a full account can be found in the published report *The Development of Writing Abilities 11-18*.

When the research project ended in 1971 the Development Project Writing across the Curriculum 11-13 was set to run for three years. Subsequently two further years were added to look at the 14-16 age range. Its brief was to disseminate the research findings and to examine the practical implications of the research theory. In *A Note on Teaching, Research and Development*, Britton wrote: 'Research findings are things we can *know* which could have a bearing on what we *do* when we teach. . . . The conclusion reached by a research team working in controlled situations cannot be directly apprehended and applied by teachers working in conditions where every variable is actively varying.'

The Development Project's work has throughout been firmly based on schools; from the start the team has worked with teachers of all subjects to try to find ways in which a pupil's writing could more effectively contribute to his personal development and learning; and not only writing but talking too as we found it impossible (and unhelpful) to ignore the interrelationship of spoken and written language. The publications from the Project have contained writing by teachers who have been keen to look for ways of employing written language more meaningfully with their students. We have learnt a good deal from them and from their efforts.

One of our aims, increasingly strongly felt as the Project nears its end, is to encourage teachers to take over responsibility for initiating discussions and setting up working groups concerned with language use in schools. The publication of the Bullock Report has given a boost to our work and there is encouraging evidence that schools are becoming more aware of the importance of a 'language across the curriculum' approach.

We hope that our book will be able to make some contribution to such discussions, especially as we have had the opportunity to document many examples of secondary students writing and talking about a wide variety of topics. Their work has been a constant source of interest and so have the contexts from which it came. In the framework that we have worked to provide for it, we hope that it will now provoke further thought, talk and even writing from a wider public audience.

References

BRITTON, J. (1970) 'Teaching, Research and Development' (unpublished)

BRITTON, J., BURGESS, T., MARTIN, N., MCLEOD, A., ROSEN, H. (1975) *The Development of Writing Abilities (11-18)* (Schools Council Research Studies) Macmillan Education

DES (1975) *A Language for Life* (Bullock Report) HMSO

SCHOOLS COUNCIL (1966) *Multiple Marking of English Compositions* Schools Council Examinations Bulletin 12 HMSO

Chapter one

The development of writing abilities

Every day in schools children write – in exercise books, in rough work books, on file paper, on worksheets. They write stories, recipes, poems, accounts of experiments; they answer questions on what they have just been told, what they have read, what they have seen or done. Why do they? What is all this writing for? What does it achieve?

When we asked pupils and students about their recent experience of writing in school we found, not surprisingly, that the teacher figured prominently in their recollections. He structures situations, he makes demands, he influences both implicitly and explicitly by his responses to what is offered. The teacher has his own ideas about what his subject is and what learning is and these inform his practice. He may be more or less aware of the criteria on which he bases his teaching but in either case his pupils soon know what pleases him. But what pleases the teacher, what he considers to be the appropriate language of his subject and the appropriate way of using it, may not be helpful – indeed may actually impede – the understanding of his pupils.

> Our history teacher used to make us put down – she gave us a load of facts to make into an essay. Well, I couldn't do that. When I was confronted with a whole list of facts I just couldn't do it and I failed my history exam and she told me I'd fail 'cos I couldn't do it.
>
> (Technical College student)

I knew what he was on about but I only knew what he was on

about in my words. I didn't know his words.

(Technical College student)

In my exams I had to change the way I learnt, you know. In all my exercise books I put it down the way I understood, but I had to remember what I'd written there and then translate it into what I think *they* will understand, you know.

(Technical College student)

At secondary school it was always writing to please whichever teacher was taking you. The fifth form was the worst for writing essays – due to the teacher we had. They all had to be very descriptive and interesting to him otherwise they were no good. If you were given a question and wrote about something completely different, this was great for him. I didn't get on very well with him so this led to low marks anyway. I managed to fool him once or twice by copying pieces out of books. This didn't always work though.

(College of Education student)

What pleases the teacher is apparently of major importance to these pupils. After all, he can be judge, jury and hangman – and there is no appeal.

The teacher as the only audience for the pupil's writing is a point which will be discussed later. Meanwhile, it is clear that if the teacher sees writing mainly as a means of recording and testing this will inevitably influence the expectations and attitudes of his pupils.

We do all the experiments. She tells us what to do and we do it and then we have to write up in our books – method, result and conclusion.

(Third year pupil)

. . . our lessons consisted entirely of bending pieces of glass over bunsen burners and copying down endless notes of dictation.

Our involvement in the learning procedure can be measured by the accuracy of my notes. Every time he dictated punctuation I wrote it down in longhand, taking 'cover' instead of 'comma' so that a sentence might read:

Common salt cover to be found in many kitchens cover is chemically made of sodium cover represented Na cover and chlorine cover represented Ch full stop

Dictation was similarly rife in other subjects.

(College of Education student)

In RS right up to the fifth year we were not allowed to make our own notes on the Apostles, everything was copied from the blackboard. This was a weekly exercise in neat writing and nothing else; we never discussed the work, nor was there any homework set. What I do not understand is why everybody passed the o level. Maybe there is some loose connection.

(College of Education student)

I don't like dictated notes because you haven't got no room for imagination. Really, when you're doing your English it's better than any other subject because you can use your imagination. You don't have to, you know, do what the teacher tells you to do.

(Fifth year pupil)

The implication that there is no room for imagination in subjects other than English might be disputed by the teachers of other subjects in that boy's school – but that is the message he has received after five years there.

What goes on in talk in the classroom may reinforce the pupil's view of how he should write:

A lot of the time, though, some of my teachers said, you know, what's your opinion and everybody gave their opinion and they said, well, that's not really right. So – you've got to take down what the teachers says in the end.

(Technical College student)

A major concern of some teachers was technical accuracy which took precedence – or so it seemed to the pupils – over content. Handwriting, spelling and punctuation were frequently referred to:

Girl 2: I like the teachers marking it but they tend to mark the spelling and the English instead of the actual story – the content.

Girl 1: Well, mostly they just mark spellings and they're so involved in getting all the spelling right that they forget the story and there's so many papers to mark they can't go over it twice.

Girl 2: And they just make sure you've got the punctuation right and everything.

(Third year pupils)

BN: What sort of things does he write?

Fiona: 'Good, but watch the punctuation' – things like that. And, um, 'Good idea, but spoilt by untidy writing'.

(Third year pupil)

The power of the teacher was dramatically illustrated by the recollections of some of the students who could remember clearly how a single remark by a particular teacher influenced their feelings about writing for months – even years – afterwards. Sometimes the effect seemed beneficial, sometimes not, but either way it seems that teachers may often underestimate the effect that their opinions can have on their pupils.

Jeanette: Well, it's mostly fairy tales I write about because Mr A – – – always commented I've got a good imagination for fairy tales, so I'm about pixies and fairies and goblins and things.

(First year girl, comprehensive school)

> BN: You said you weren't any good at it (writing poems), didn't you?
>
> Sandra: No, I'm not very good at it.
>
> BN: Now why do you say that?
>
> Sandra: Because when I was at primary school I got a very low mark for a poem that I'd done and the teacher put underneath it: poetry isn't your bright spark, or something, is it? And that's what put me off, I think.

> (Third year girl, comprehensive school)

My first notion of the change in emphasis between junior and grammar school came when I had to write an essay on Neolithic man for my first piece of history homework. I started 'My name is Wanda and I am the son of the headman in our village.' The history master read it out to the rest of the class in a sarcastic voice – everybody laughed and I felt deeply humiliated. I got 3/20 for covering the page with writing. I hated history after that until the third year.

> (College of Education student)

The influence of the teacher, then, may be profound and is certainly pervasive. All the more reason why he should be as fully aware as possible of the options open to him in approaching his pupils' writing – in what he asks them to do and in how he responds to what they have done. But the opportunities for children to use writing more effectively can be widened much more than this. If the teacher is concerned not only with *what* he asks his pupils to do but also with *how* he allows them to respond (after all, why shouldn't a history homework on Neolithic man begin 'My name is Wanda ...'?) then he may find that they discover their own strategies for learning through writing. And if he also allows opportunities for pupils to write for an audience other than himself – perhaps the class – then his pupils' opportunities to experience different writing situations will have been significantly widened.

The development of writing abilities

What is the writing for? Who is it for? These were the two questions to which the research team of the Schools Council Project The Written Language of 11-18 Year Olds chiefly addressed themselves when they looked at a sample of about 2000 pieces of school writing which they had collected from 65 secondary schools. They wanted to find a way of describing how writing was used in schools so that they could go on to define or track any development in writing abilities (Britton *et al* 1975).

To do this, the Project developed in detail these two dimensions of writing: 'Sense of audience' (*who* the writing was for) and 'Function' (*what* it was for). Other dimensions are, of course, possible, and the research team looked at, for instance, individual language resources. The results of their analysis of the 2000 pieces of school writing and the implications which they drew from their results are the foundations upon which the Development Project Writing across the Curriculum 11–16 has worked.

The research team not only listed the different kinds of writing but they also looked for the relationships between them. They made specific suggestions about the way writing ability develops, about the order of development and the reasons for it. They suggested the relationships between the different functions of writing, the audience for which they were written and the mental processes required to produce them. In fact, they provided an approach which is valid for all areas of the curriculum – a 'writing across the curriculum' rationale.

So before presenting some of the work of the Development Project we need to summarize the model for looking at writing which the research team formulated.

A sense of audience – the child and his reader

A sense of audience – how the writer pictures his reader – is obviously very important in determining how the writing is done. A letter to a friend, to an acquaintance, to a newspaper may all be about the same subject but will be very differently written by any competent writer. Furthermore, another letter to the same friend on a different occasion may differ markedly from the first. If, for example, the first letter was to inform your friend about certain social events in which you knew he was interested and the second was to persuade him to take a particular course of action which you thought he might be reluctant to do, then you will be seeing your reader in different ways.

In school children write mostly for the teacher. But what makes for differences between pieces of writing is not just who the reader is but how the writer *sees* his reader. Different children see the same teacher in different ways, of course. But a child may also see his teacher as a different sort of reader on different occasions. (Sometimes teachers may make this explicit to the children – '. . . she doesn't care about the English side when we're writing stories. She just marks the story itself. But when we're told that she's going to mark the punctuation and that, y'know, it's all right then' – Third year girl, comprehensive school.)

In distinguishing between the different sorts of 'sense of audience' found in school writing, the writing research team suggested these main categories (for a fuller account of audience categories see Britton *et al* 1975):

1 Child (or adolescent) to self
2 Child (or adolescent) to trusted adult
3 Pupil to teacher as partner in dialogue
4 Pupil to teacher seen as examiner or assessor
5 Child (or adolescent) to his peers (as expert, co-worker, friend, etc.)
6 Writer to his readers (or unknown audience)

1 'Child to self' writing takes no account of the needs of any other reader – as in some diaries, notes and first drafts.
2 Writing for the teacher could come under any of the categories 2–4. In 'Child to trusted adult' the writing takes place because the reader exists for it who can be relied on to respond sympathetically. So the child may write about personal, deeply felt matters which he would not attempt to do without feeling very secure with his reader. For example:

> If I think about what I would really like to do, I feel as if I want to curl into a ball and let everything go on without me. Knowing about it. Whichever way I turn, I feel trapped. College doesn't seem a release, it seems a new trap, another place where I have to conform to something . . .
>
> (Carol 18)

3 'Pupil to teacher as partner in dialogue' covers writing which is recognisably part of an educational process. Here the dialogue is likely to be centrally concerned with the subject matter of school, although the writer's personal feelings about it may be included. The child still feels secure in the teacher's presence and is assuming that the teacher is there to help him, will be interested in what he is saying and is likely to respond to what he writes – hence, 'dialogue'. For example:

. . . If we look back through history at any one incident if that did not happen or if something else happened instead we could have a totally different way of life. I think that any main discisions that are taken should be aimed at the future. So it will not affect the future population in any ways that would harm their ways of life. Political discussions are very important to the future. If China was allowed to join the UN this could help the future tremendesly.

(John 14: 'China and the UN')

4 'Pupil to teacher seen as examiner or assessor' refers not only to exams but to all writing which the child appears to be producing simply to satisfy a teacher's demand and on which he expects to be judged or assessed – either for how well he has written or for what he has shown he knows. For example:

Tamworth was Peel's own consitutency. All the Tamworth Manifesto was, was what Peel said the Tories (or conservatives) would do. He said that Tories would support the Reform act and would not let past grievances exist any longer. These were the two most important things that Peel said, as they have been the Conservatives word upto this day and have not yet been broken.

(Janet 15: The Tamworth Manifesto)

5 'Child (or adolescent) to his peers (as expert, co-worker, friend etc.)'. Although the teacher may be a member of the audience for writing in this category, the focus is upon the peer group. For example:

> The rooms were changed a lot and so also was Mr Comer. The way the rooms were changed was. The benches were in different orders and Mr Comers desk was pushed back to the blackboard. . . '. Mr Comer was changed a lot two. The ways he was changed were, there was no 'are you at your bench' or no 'go to your bench and stay at it' or no 'Stay! at your bench.' Mr Comer also was going round giveing more of a helping hand than usual. The boys talked to Mr Comer about the job and he wasn't the usual old cross look-ing black patch, He was happy took a joke and listend to a joke. If any-body was doing anything wrong he didn't catch them by the ear and blow his top, instead he told them where they were wrong and explined how to do it. Thes effects weren't of him on the following Monday.

> (Cyril 12: reporting to his classmates about a woodwork lesson which he had observed in his school)

6 'Writer to his readers (or unknown audience)'. Writing for an unknown or public audience expresses the writer's sense of the general value of what he has to say, and that he is not addressing himself to any particular audience. Some school writing comes into this category. For example:

> . . . A child quarrels in order to assert itself, and frequently fails to do so. Its main desire is to have supremacy over something. It cannot, in all probability, have any power over an adult and so has to find its power in breaking things or being the leader of a gang. This wish stems from the animal kingdom, where survival of the fittest means that only the

strongest, most powerful are successful. Animals only fight over serious matters, like where to live, and what to eat.

(Derek 15)

The research team classified their sample of scripts in terms of 'sense of audience' as follows:

Audience by year (percentages of year sample)

	Year 1	Year 3	Year 5	Year 7
Self	0	0	0	0
Trusted adult	2	3	2	1
Pupil-teacher dialogue	51	45	36	19
Teacher examiner	40	45	52	61
Peer group	0	0	0	0
Public	0	1	5	6
Miscellaneous (translation, dictation, exercises etc.)	7	6	5	13

Audience by subject (percentages of subject sample)

	English	History	Geography	RE	Science
Self*	0	0	0	0	0
Trusted adult	5	0	0	4	0
Pupil-teacher dialogue	65	17	13	64	7
Teacher examiner	18	69	81	22	87
Peer group	0	0	0	0	0
Public	6	0	0	0	0
Miscellaneous	6	14	6	10	6

*(The team considered that in any involved writing the self was a significant part of the writer's sense of audience. They therefore defined the category for their purposes as covering items obviously unconnected with an audience – rough work for instance.)

What is most striking about these figures is that writing for the 'Examiner' audience accounts for about half of all school writing.

Even in the first year it was 40%. This does not necessarily mean that teachers *intended* the situation to be one of examination or assessment – but that is how the pupils saw the context for their writing. As we saw earlier, the way the teacher responds to writing will determine how the pupil sees the situation. And, of course, previous experience in school will set up expectations about writing. In addition it may also be that the whole atmosphere of the secondary school promotes the sense of constantly being assessed.

What this means, though, is that the single most important use for writing in secondary schools appears to be as a means of testing and not as a means of learning – and that this emphasis becomes stronger as the child moves up the school.

Of course teachers must assess their pupils' progress. But that so much of secondary school writing appears to be concerned with assessment is worrying because it suggests that the more important function of writing – its potential contribution to the mental, emotional and social development of the writer – is being neglected.

The emphasis on testing, on monitoring knowledge and performance, which the research figures indicate, suggests that most school writing is seen not as part of the learning process but as something which happens *after* the learning.

However, before looking at some examples of what effect changing the 'sense of audience' can have on writing in schools, we need to look at the second of the two dimensions developed by the writing research team, because then we can see how they interrelate.

Functions of writing

Another major influence on the writer is his sense of what the writing is for. Our culture has developed distinct language forms which are typically associated with certain situations. For example, we know when we are listening to a story, or a speech, or are being persuaded to buy something – because we have internalised these kinds of language from our day-to-day encounters with them. When children come to write they draw on their pool of language experience which helps them to know what kind of language to use in certain types of situation. For instance, few children in an infant class are taught to begin their stories 'Once upon a time' or 'Once there was a . . .', but most of them do this because this beginning is so clear a 'marker' of stories which they have listened to or read.

Although the boundaries are not clear-cut, the writing research team suggested three broad categories of function to which recognisably distinct kinds of writing belong. What distinguishes them is that both writer and reader recognise the conventions that distinguish one 'job' from another. There are often linguistic differences, too, and these are indicators of the different functions – but the essential difference lies in the sorts of things the writer *takes for granted about his reader's response*. If, for instance, we read 'Once upon a time there was a flying horse', we know the writer is taking it for granted that we shall recognise a story and shall not quarrel about whether horses can fly. On the other hand, if we read 'The biggest aircraft company in America is the Northrop Corporation, trade name Boeing . . . ', we might reasonably dispute this and refer to evidence which indicated that there was a larger aircraft company in America. But if we read 'When I write it is as if all the ideas in my head have come together into order and when I write I am reading them for the first time . . . ', we recognise that the writer is assuming that we are interested in her and in her experience.

The three 'recognised and allowed for' functions of writing are represented by the research team as a continuum thus:

Transactional ← Expressive → Poetic

The characteristics of each function can be defined as follows:

Expressive: in which it is taken for granted that the writer himself is of interest to the reader; he feels free to jump from facts to speculation to personal anecdote to emotional outburst and none of it will be taken down and used against him – it is all part of being a person *vis à vis* another person. It is the means by which the new is tentatively explored, thoughts may be half-uttered, attitudes half-expressed, the rest being left to be picked up by a listener or reader who is willing to take the unexpressed on trust.

The following extract from a personal log book written by Andrew, aged 12, illustrates many of the features of expressive writing:

Before what I'm about to write Mr T . . . told us what to do. It took a bit of getting through to some of the class and as they didn't understand they became restless and Mr T . . . had to interrupt what he was saying and deal with them. He shouldn't have to do this because they should know that if they don't understand they should listen again to what he is saying and perhaps they'll know what he's talking about. The student teacher who worked with us in English and Enquiry is quite a nice woman and she helps us do our work, she has a good voice when reading aloud and you can understand her. When the class starts throwing pencils over an argument, she gets upset and sometimes leaves the room, I think she should be much firmer with the class and then with a bit of luck they might obey her, but still, she's doing all right. Oh, by the way I suppose you're wondering what her name is, it's Miss M . . . In Enquiry I think I've done well and I am satisfied with what I have done. At the beginning of the Enquiry work we went to Burgh Hill farm. Visiting the farm and looking round was very interesting and I enjoyed it very much, I can't say that much for the journey as I was sick, at least four times, twice going, twice coming back. All the other work we did is at the top of the page, it's not because I am to busy to right them down, I can just write about some of them as I go along.

This writing is very like written down speech, reflecting the ebb and flow of the writer's thoughts and feelings – and this is what expressive language (spoken or written) does. Speech is always on the move: it moves according to the demands of what it is for, what the listener wants to hear, and how the speaker's language resources allow him to meet these demands – his own and other people's. So expressive speech shuttles to and fro and expressive writing can be seen to move in a similar way.

Transactional: in which it is taken for granted that the writer means what he says and can be challenged for its truthfulness to public knowledge, and for its logicality; that it claims to be able to stand on its own and does not derive its validity from coming from a particular person. So it is the typical language of science and of intellectual inquiry, of technology, of trade, of planning, reporting, instructing, informing, advising, persuading, arguing and theorising. It is also the language most used in school writing.

> Greater London Council Ambulance Service was built in 1969. Before it was built for them there was a place called the Red Cross. The red Cross was made into a private service for all over the country. But even before that there was a place called Cadogan Iron Foundry. There is a peculiar pipe system in the building now, it is a heating system. The pipes come from the RAF runway which they used these pipes for burning lots of paraffin to clear the fog and so the planes can see the runway.
>
> (Nigel 12: writing for Local Studies)

Poetic: in which it is taken for granted that 'true or false?' is not a relevant question at the literal level. What is presented may or may not in fact be a representation of actual reality but the writer takes it for granted that his reader will *experience* what is presented rather in the way he experiences his own memories, and not use it like a guidebook or map in his dealings with the world. When Huck Finn said that all Tom Sawyer's stories were lies he was mistaking the function of stories (the poetic function) and operating the 'rules' of the other 'game' – the transactional. So a reader does different things with transactional and poetic writings: he *uses* transactional writing, or any part of it, but who can say what we do with a story or a poem that we read, or a play we watch? Perhaps we just share it with the writer; and not having to 'do' anything with it leaves us free to attend to its formal features – which are more implicit than explicit – the pattern of events in a narrative, the configuration of an idea, above all the pattern of feelings evoked: in attending in this noninstrumental way we experience feelings and values as part of what we are sharing. Writing in the poetic function shows a heightened awareness of symbolic, aural and even visual qualities – of *shaping* a verbal construct – as in this story by Eleanor, aged 6:

The prince and the princes
Once upon a time the was a prince and he whent for a ride on his horse. and he went past a castle and sore the most beautiful

princess in the whole wide woled and the prince said please will you mary me. but the princesses mummy wode not let her mary the prince so one day the priness saied I am going for a rid on my hores so of she went but realy she went to go and cellect the prince and thay went to another contre and gote mared and lived happily ever after.

The end.

Growth from the expressive

The expressive is basic. Expressive speech is how we communicate with each other most of the time and expressive writing, being the form of writing nearest to speech, is crucial for trying out and coming to terms with new ideas. Because it is the kind of writing in which we most fully reveal ourselves to our reader – in a trusting relationship – it is instrumental in setting up a dialogue between writer and reader from which both can learn.

Expressive writing we think is the seed bed from which more specialised and differentiated kinds of writing can grow – towards the greater explicitness of the transactional or the more conscious shaping of the poetic.

Much effective writing seems to be on a continuum somewhere between the expressive and the transactional or somewhere between the expressive and the poetic. This applies to adult as well as children's writing. What is worrying is that in much school writing the pupil is expected to exclude expressive features and to present his work in an unexpressive transactional mode. The demand for impersonal, unexpressive writing can actively inhibit learning because it isolates what is to be learned from the vital learning process – that of making links between what is already known and the new information.

Believing, then, in the central importance of the expressive both in learning and in learning to write, it is hardly surprising that the writing research team were perturbed by the results of their analysis of the school writing which they had collected. The figures (percentages) were as follows:

Function by year

	Year 1	Year 3	Year 5	Year 7
Transactional	54	57	62	84
Expressive	6	6	5	4
Poetic	17	23	24	7
Miscellaneous	23	14	9	5

Function by subject

	English	History	Geography	RE	Science
Transactional	34	88	88	57	92
Expressive	11	0	0	11	0
Poetic	39	2	0	12	0
Miscellaneous	16	10	12	20	8

These figures suggest that most secondary school writing is *transactional* and that it becomes increasingly so as the pupils move up the school. If we put these figures beside those for 'sense of audience' quoted earlier, we have a picture of secondary school writing which begins as largely transactional, written for a teacher who is going to assess it, and that as pupils get older this becomes even more exclusively the way that they are required to write.

The expressive function, which the writing research team saw as so important, accounts for a mere 6% of school writing in Year 1, declining to 4% by Year 7.

But if the bulk of school writing is transactional, what sort of things are pupils writing? The informational subcategories of this function, which represent a scale of distance from an actual event, give an idea of the range of possibilities:

Transactional

Informational   *Conative*

1 Record: what is happening
2 Report: what happened   1 Regulative
3 Generalised narrative or description ⎤ what   2 Persuasive
4 Low level generalisation   ⎬ generally
5 Generalisation – classification   ⎦ happens
6 Speculation ⎤ what may
7 Theorising ⎦ happen

However, up to the end of the fifth year almost all the transactional writing in the sample fell into the first five informational categories. Rarely was there any sense that they were taking part in a dialogue in which new ideas could be aired and explored. The writing, in most cases, was seen as an end product – an account of something that had already happened.

There was hardly any writing by pupils younger than sixteen which could be categorised as speculative, theoretical or persuasive. This was not because such pupils are incapable of writing in these ways but because they were not given opportunities to do so.

The research team commented: '. . . for whatever reason, curricular aims did not include the fostering of writing that reflects independent thinking: rather attention was directed towards classificatory writing which reflects information in the form in which both teacher and textbook traditionally present it.'

An example of the kind of speculative writing which was rare in the sample collected by the Research Project is this piece which is the last page of Nigel's CSE Project, 'Making alcohol from waste paper'. Nigel was not asked to present his project in any given way.

My project worked very well and I'm pleased because 1) I got alcohol from paper which I throught was never possible, 2) because I used some new equipment which I've never herd of let alone worked with. Another thing, I was pleased about was there was lots of experments and if there was anything I wanted to know there was book's at my finger tips so there wern't any time lost. If I had a lot more time what I would like to make is a lot more alcohol and do lots of flame tests because I only made about 1cm of pure alcohol. So I could not do much, I would allso like to find how much yeast is necessary to ferment it propley yet let the alcohol burn propley. I would also like to know if it was the yeast that stoped it burning. I would also like to learn how to control the heat when distilling because thats a mistake I made.

(Nigel 15)

Nigel is not only assessing for himself what he has achieved but he is also generating his own questions for further enquiry. His teacher commented: 'His enthusiasm and pleasure derived from the project is refreshing, but more important throughout there is evidence of clear scientific thinking in Nigel's own words.'

Genuine communication

The trouble with most school writing is that it is not genuine communication. When adults write they are usually trying to tell someone something he doesn't already know; when children write in school they are usually writing for someone who, they are well aware, knows better than they do what they are trying to say and who is concerned to evaluate their attempt to say it. Even when they are writing a story, when the teacher does not know better than they do what they are saying, the response of the teacher is so often to the surface features of spelling, punctuation and handwriting. So once again the teacher is seen as an assessor and not as someone interested in being communicated with.

If the bulk of school writing is transactional (and of limited range from the transactional at that), and if much of what is not transactional is marked by the teacher for its technical accuracy, rather than responded to for its content, then only a small part of the possible range of writing purposes is fostered and there is limited opportunity for development.

The teacher's role is of great significance here. Pupils cannot operate a range of functions for a teacher who evaluates narrowly whatever is produced. Thus if an English teacher asks his pupils to write a letter to a local newspaper intending to give them the opportunity to write transactionally for a public audience and yet the pupils know that not only will the 'letters' go no further than the teacher but that he will correct their spelling etc, then this task is a bogus one and the pupils will be writing, yet again, to please the teacher. There are two ways out of this impasse. Either the teacher must find other audiences than himself for what the children write or he must agree to be communicated with as someone other than an assessor, or both. This means he must change his way of responding and this has social as well as pedagogic implications.

When we asked students to recall any of their school writing with which they had felt satisfied, it was clear that the sense of audience often played an important part in making the writing experience memorable – as in this example:

The most satisfying piece of writing I have wrote was when I was reporting on the school's Rugby for the school magazine. Every week I wrote a small report on the Saturday match and worked out average points per match and how many games we had won and lost.

At the end of the season a few of the match reports were put into the yearly magazine and also the facts and figures. I also gave each player (except myself) a mark out of ten for each match. In the end the best player to my way of thinking got an average of just over eight out of ten per match. The season was a successful one for our team, we won eighteen matches and lost only three, our average points per game were sixteen with only four against per match.

(Technical College student)

The enthusiasm for this writing can still be felt in the recollection of it and the student's desire to tell us the results of his calculations. And yet he didn't do this writing as a part of school 'work' but as an extra related to something he was obviously keen on – playing rugby. In addition, and equally important, he was writing for an audience who wanted to read what he wrote. So the student was writing a 'genuine communication' about something which interested him for a real audience who were also interested in what he wrote.

What happened to their writing was also very important to these students:

The only other piece of writing I've done which sticks out in my memory was a poem I wrote at school. I can't remember now what it was about, but I do know it was printed in the school magazine.

My most satisfying piece of work was a poem I wrote when I was about fourteen. When I had finished it, I felt extreemly satisfyed for some strange reason, mainly because it rymed well and had a meaning. It was also published in the school magazine which I thought was rather good.

The pleasure of seeing one's name in print along with one's special story made up for all the worry of putting the story together.

(Technical College students)

Contrast those recollections with the comments below by intending teachers who were asked to write about whatever they could remember of the writing they did at school:

In my fourth year mock o level Eng. Lang. I was penalised for writing an essay that was too long on a description of a building. The master told me that it was wrong to get too interested in a subject and said that I could do that after I left school; by then I didn't care anyway, I did the same thing in the exam and got a grade 1. I still have reams of poems at home that I never took to school because I didn't think it was to do with school.
In secondary school my English came under violent attack by a whole series of teachers. . . . The head thought I was dyslectic (never can spell even now). I think I just hated writting or rather I actually enjoyed writting untill work was returned to me with such red lines and a poor grade.

(College of Education students)

A first year girl in a comprehensive school makes a similar point:

Only thing is, the problem when you get it back there's a cross by it.

A fourth year boy was more explicit. He wrote:

When I get a piece of work back and I think its good and I get a bad mark I feel like frotiling the teacher.

When school writing in all subjects is marked chiefly for accuracy – either of content or form, or both – then pupils are constantly in a testing situation where they will take the minimum of risks. They don't want to make mistakes. So they will try to use the language which has been given to them – by the teacher or the textbook – and not their own language. They will be cautious and will try to disguise any lack of understanding if they are aware of it. But by not taking chances, by not trying things out in their own language, by not attempting to make connections between their own experience or knowledge and the new information that they are acquiring, they are being limited in their opportunities for growth.

Understanding new information means relating it to what we already 'know' – fitting it in to our view of how things are. So it will often mean not just giving an account of something but expressing a response to it – as in the following extract from a personal log book written by Kenneth, a 12 year old boy in a London comprehensive school. The log book is a kind of diary in which the pupils write their thoughts about their work and related subjects. The teacher reads it and writes back. He does not evaluate or 'correct' their writing:

This term I've learnt about the country side after are visit to burghill farm in sussex from which I learnt alot how the cows were milked and how it was transport it to the tanker. And enclosers which effected people's life. I learnt about iron, conditions of work, mines power and inventions. I fell that I have learnt a lot than I did in my primary school. I enjoy english and enquiry but some times it's hard to think like know because people are chattering away happily. I learn by listening to the teacher and reading books I think about it then write it in my own words. I think that the class should be split into half (the people who want to work and the people who don't). But I must be honest some time's me and robert stop working for a minute or two and have a chat after some hard work then we start work again. I am most interested in english when we do play's but I think that to many people write plays and every one starts shouting and arguring. I think that I work quite good as I enjoy my work. I think that the industrial revolation changed alot of peoples life's like Willaim Wilkins when his land was taken away from him by the squire and had it enclosed. He had to change the whole of his life style. He had to grow extra food to live on then he sold it to Nottingham the nearest town. I don't think it's fare to change the life style you alway's know just for the squire and a few rich farmers. The working conditions of 18th century life was terrible having to live in four rooms and going to a out sick (?), and children from the age of 5 having to go to work in factorys and mines.

Much of this is expressive, close to talk, but it also carries information, as well as the response to it. Kenneth speculates about how to improve his own working conditions by splitting the class in half – the people who want to work and the people who don't – and then realises that this division may not always be easy to recognise: 'But I must be honest some time's me and robert stop working for a minute or two and have a chat after some hard work then we start work again.' So through the writing Kenneth is working out his own view of things.

Another way of understanding information is to do something with it – as opposed to just recording or reporting it. David, another second year comprehensive school pupil, was invited by his history teacher to write the speech that a wealthy landowner might have made to persuade villagers to accept enclosures:

Lisiten to your trusted squire for if you lisiten your land will grow and your children will grow healthy. If your don't you will suffer badly and children will grow up to be unhealthy. I gather you have heard of enclosures. I reckon they are a very good idea, for if we have strips of land we waste time by going from one strip to another strips but if we have enclosures we save time and crops will grow bigger and the land will be bigger. Suddenly you will grow healthy and wealthy and your children will be so wealthy they will be able to stand in my position so will your trust me. When your have your harvest next year you will see that your crops grow bigger and better and you will even come and tell me. Thank you for lisitening. A roar comes from the poor landowners.

David is using the information he has been given about enclosures – what they were, that the wealthy benefited from them and that the poor did not – and has tried to show how a wealthy landowner might have presented this information to suit himself. The exaggerated promise 'you will grow healthy and wealthy' reminds us of advertising copy. David's final sentence, 'A roar comes from the poor landowners' is neatly ironic. The writing is for an imagined public audience but it is not the dead language so often found in textbooks.

To sum up
The writing research team asked two questions: Who is the writing for? What is it for? We think that these are important questions for teachers to ask themselves about any writing they expect their pupils to do. As a Development Project that is one of our main concerns – to offer teachers the way of looking at the writing process which the research project formulated. Arising from this we hope we can:

1 encourage teachers *of all subjects* to provide a variety of audiences for their pupils' writing so that they are not so often seen as the teacher-examiner who evaluates whatever the pupils write;
2 encourage teachers *of all subjects* to provide for their pupils a range of writing purposes (linked to a range of audiences) so that pupils are given more opportunity to express their thoughts on paper in a variety of ways – expressive, transactional and poetic;
3 encourage the use of written language as well as spoken for a wider range of thought processes: interpreting, reflecting, thinking creatively and speculatively, as well as recording, reporting, generalising and classifying;
4 encourage teachers of all subjects to discuss together how language (spoken and written) can most effectively help their pupils to learn.

References
BRITTON, J., BURGESS, T., MARTIN, N., MCLEOD, A., ROSEN, H. (1975) *The Development of Writing Abilities (11-18)* (Schools Council Research Studies) Macmillan Education

Chapter two

From talking to writing

Although the main focus of the Development Project's work has necessarily been on the use made by students and teachers of writing, as we said in our introduction we have found it impossible, and undesirable, to ignore the opportunities for talk which also occur across the curriculum. Neither form of language at secondary level can be used for long to the exclusion of the other; indeed our own view would be that many learning situations could often be improved if the two were more closely interrelated. That is why our concern in this chapter is primarily with talk, the audiences that exist for it and the purposes it can serve when children go to school, because the ways in which pupils learn to learn through spoken language may be of immense value when they come in the later years of their schooling to use written language as an indispensable mode of acquiring knowledge.

What is talking for?
Most children learn to talk long before they ever come to school because they need to, very powerfully. From birth onwards there are an ever increasing number of reasons connected with the individual's own growth and development that render speech absolutely necessary to him; as soon as he can, therefore, the young child *makes talk work for him* in a whole variety of ways.

We know now that children from all countries and cultures learn to talk at approximately the same age – between 18 and 30 months – and that well before that they have already been burbling sounds in the intonation patterns of their native language. We know also that the patterns of language learning in all young children are very similar: they learn the same kinds of words first, construct the same kinds of telegraphic sentences next and begin to expand these into longer sentences again at about the same age and in about the same ways.

Researchers have told us a lot about how we learn to talk. For us, though, a more important question is what does talking do for us or enable us to do? We would like to summarize some of the possibilities. It is widely believed that children are initially motivated to talk by the need to communicate to the adults who care for them, especially their mothers, what their needs are – for food, warmth, comfort, stimulation and so forth. Well before they can shape sounds into words, babies use their voices to express satisfaction or dissatisfaction about how they feel.

Another theory holds that children learn to talk in order to get closer to the adults around them. They sense somehow that these adults are using sounds to establish and maintain relationships and they experience how their own sound-making brings responses. They quickly discover, for example, that they can get loving, approving responses from these adults by imitating certain sounds that the adults are making.

After a while this use of talk to get closer to parents and other important members of the family naturally extends into talk used to become more oneself – different from other people. We can say that this is language used for the development of individual identity: who I am, as against who I am not.

More or less simultaneously, children begin to use talk also to understand how and why things happen – partly out of curiosity and partly out of sheer practical necessity. Sometimes, for instance, talk may be used to help understand what happens when a favourite toy is dropped down the stairs. Other talk is used to understand more abstract things like where daddy goes when he leaves the house every morning. As James Britton has illustrated so vividly in *Language and Learning*, in all of this children are also learning to use the language itself to carry or represent the experience, without always needing the actual thing in front of them to refer to. Embedded in this use of talk to understand how and why things happen as they do – to make interpretations of past and present experiences – is the impulse to predict what will happen in new situations.

In addition, small children take great delight at times in simply playing with spoken language, making words the material of play in the way that a ball or a stick or a stuffed toy might be. All children, given the opportunity, find pure pleasure in making 'things' with words and all, as Ruth Weir has pointed out in *Language in the Crib*, use this play to practise their talking competencies and to extend them into new areas. Chanting nonsense syllables, nursery rhymes, skipping games and so on still has a universal fascination for children.

To summarize briefly, talk enables us to

1 communicate our basic physiological needs
2 establish and maintain social relationships
3 develop and maintain our unique identity
4 understand how and why things happen as they do
5 predict what will happen in new situations
6 have fun – sheer sensual and aesthetic pleasure.

Talk structured by the teacher

What we now want to ask is how far all these basic motivations continue to be fulfilled through talk when children go to school, especially at secondary level. We realise that in any situation motives for using language will be mixed and that it would be a mistake to try and plan talk in lessons specifically for this motive or that. But we also believe that if these purposes are not catered for in school talk, it will become for pupils a somewhat pointless exercise – both their own utterances and those of their teachers.

From studies of classroom language we know that in general at secondary level, teachers tend to control classroom talk very tightly. Often it is their questions rather than questions from the pupils that structure the discussion; the teacher's responses to answers received from the class are in consequence strongly influenced by his intention to elicit specific information. At the time of writing this chapter an article appeared in the *Education Guardian* giving this advice to new teachers: 'Not all pupil questions are requests for information, and though you may be deeply moved by the up-raised hand, earnest face, and ever-so-sincere voice, do not judge by appearances . . .'.

The tone is semibantering but the implication is clear – it is the teacher's job to ask the questions and any from the class are to be regarded with suspicion because they will almost certainly deflect him from his own structure for the lesson. As a quick reminder of the flavour and the feel of this kind of classroom talk, which can hardly be called either a conversation or a discussion, here is one of the teacher-pupil interchanges from *Language, the Learner and the School*: the teacher was explaining that milk is an example of the suspension of solids in a liquid:

T: You get the white . . . what we call casein . . . that's . . . er . . . protein . . . which is good for you . . . it'll help to build bones . . . and the white is mainly the casein and so it's not actually a solution . . . it's a suspension of very fine particles together with water and various other things which are dissolved in water. . . .

P1: Sir, at my old school I shook my bottle of milk up and when I looked at it again all the sides was covered with . . . er . . . like particles and . . . er . . . could they be the white particles in the milk . . .?

P2: Yes, and gradually they would sediment out wouldn't they, to the bottom . . .?

P3: When milk goes very sour though it smells like cheese, doesn't it?

P4: Well it is cheese isn't it, if you leave it long enough?

T: Anyway can we get on. . . . We'll leave a few questions for later.

Where the classroom context for the talk is dominantly pre-scriptive in the sense that it is chiefly the teacher who is doing the telling, inevitably the pupils are given very little opportunity to do more than listen as best they can, or to have their own offerings dismissed, or to slot in the appropriate word or phrase when the teacher pauses for them to do so. In this kind of situation both the talk and the writing are produced primarily to please the teacher – as some of the comments that we quoted in chapter one reflected very clearly: 'She tells us what to do and we do it and then we have to write it up in our books . . .', '. . . you've got to take down what the teacher says in the end.'

Teachers as listeners
It can make a crucial difference when the teacher is prepared to be

a good listener as well as a fluent talker. By definition almost, where this is the case the learning context becomes more co-operative because there is scope in it for the pupils to make genuine contributions of their own and to follow the thread of their own thoughts instead of trying most of the time to guess what is in the teacher's mind.

We have no doubt from our conversations with pupils in many schools that they value and appreciate teachers who listen and pay serious rather than sceptical attention to what they have to say: 'I sit in the classroom and you know, just talk or discuss things with J or any teacher who happens to be around. I like discussing things, I find it very useful, I talk to anybody.' The same boy, whose work we have used extensively in one of our pamphlets, also recollected how different the situation was at his previous school where he felt that his own opinions would have been discounted:

By the time I left my other school I was getting rather low in the opinions of the teachers – 'cos I disagreed with what they were saying – you know – one teacher said that colour prejudice, to be colour prejudiced was natural and everyone was, and I disagreed with that and I didn't dare tell him so – so I was just stroppy with him. . . . At that school they just didn't talk to teachers – a couple of words with a sir at the end and that was it. At the moment, talking to teachers I can express my opinions and – you know it doesn't matter if it conflicts with anybody else's opinion, nobody takes it like a personal grudge – and it's very useful 'cos you can just talk in terms of what you're arguing about, and argue about it without the teacher thinking that you're being cheeky or stupid or anything like that.

The piece of talk which follows was made possible because Pete (who was in an ESN unit with an IQ of less than 70 at the age of fourteen), had a teacher who understood the need to provide him with an interested and attentive audience. Because this teacher was willing to spend a long time listening, Pete was able to discover how much he actually knew inside his own head about one of his consuming interests, dinosaurs. In the telling, he has to struggle to reshape what he knows in the way that many more literate children have to do in writing:

T: Your hobby, Pete, is dinosaurs . . . dinosaurs and airplanes and ships. Tell us about dinosaurs . . . what is a dinosaur?

P: A dinosaur is a creature with a little brain and has legs. The first one was the brontosaurus. He was a stupid fellow. Brontosaurus lived many years ago . . . before man. Brontosaurus was so clumsy he probably could not walk. Brontosaurus was 70 feet long, and he had a brain in his tail to balance him. The other one was a tyrannosaurus. He was a tyrant king.

T: Is that what it means, tyrannosaurus?

P: Yes, tyrannosaurus was a tyrant king. It was so fierce you could not stop the tyrannosaurus rex. The tyrannosaurus rex is 20 feet and 50 feet long.

T: You said he was 20 feet and 50 feet tall. I didn't quite understand.

P: His tail was long.

T: How long was his tail?

P: 50 feet.

T: Yeah, and he was 20 feet tall?

P: Yeah.

T: Sorry.

P: The tyrannosaurus had teeth of two feet long . . . that long. The other one was a triceratops. We called it triceratops because it had three horns. It was a big dinosaur 'cause it had a beak on the end of its, uh, face. The triceratops had big horns and it faced its enemies and it defend itself. The triceratops did not, could not, go in the water, because it was so scared it could not go in the water. The triceratops was a creature with a ? on its front.

T: A what?

P: A ? on its front.

T: Oh, yes.

P: The triceratops was . . . (Pete can't remember what he wants to say; the teacher says to go on.) The other one is a stegosaurus. We call it stegosaurus because it had so many shells on it, so many shells on it, because it was ?, because stegosaurus was a plant-eater. Stegosaurus protect itself by its tail. The tail hits other dinosaurs with 'em. Stegosaurus had a little brain. He was so close to the ground he could not walk properly, but he was so clumsy and he had a brain in his tail and he lived in muddy swamps and it defend itself because it had a good tail to hit with. The tail has four forks sticking out of it to hit dinosaurs with it. The other one is called a platiosaurus. The platiosaurus was 20 feet same as tyrannosaurus. He stand on his feet. The platiosaurus his tail was 50 feet long, same as the tyrannosaurus. Platiosaurus lived in many swamps but he was a plant-eater. Platiosaurus he had teeth of 2 feet long. Platiosaurus had a big head, big as a tyrannosaurus' head. It was so big it was nearly big as a window frame. The platiosaurus had big hands, small, he could pick up . . . he could not fight properly . . .

T: Wait a minute, he had big hands and small? Which?

P: He had small hands and big arms . . . the other one, the ephalophosaurus was a plant-eater. It had a bump on his head, a crest. It was called a crest dinosaur because he was 40 feet . . . um. . . . Ephalophosaurus he was ever so big that he stood 40 feet, and the ephalophosaurus lived in Jurassic times. He was more hundred years ago . . . hundreds of years ago. The ephalophosaurus had big claws and stayed in many swamps. He had a brain in his tail and it defend its enemies. It used to fight the tyrannosaurus and its best enemy was the tyrannosaurus and the . . . um . . . megalosaurus and the . . . um . . . uh . . . it defend itself . . . um . . . ˙

T: That's O.K., that's all right, that's fine, fine . . .

P: His other enemy was the stegosaurus . . .

T: Let's stop there a minute, Pete, will you? Just a second. (The tape is shut off, then on again.)

T: Pete, that was marvellous. Tell me, where'd you get all that information from?

P: 'Cause I was so interested in 'em.

T: Yes, what did you do?

P: I brought models in, of 'em, and I made tons of 'em.

T: Kits that you buy?

P: Yeah.

T: Well, where did you find out all about them, you know, what they were like?

P: Yes, they came out of the sea . . . and came up on land.

T: Yes, but where did you find out about this, in books?

P: I found it out in books and on television.

T: You don't read very well, Pete, do you?

P: No.

T: So did someone read to you, or you kept asking questions?

P: Usually I asked my dad, and my dad usually reads stories about them.

T: Did you ask Mrs P occasionally?

P: Yes.

T: Did you do some work in school on them?

P: Yes, I've got a project on them. I did have a project on 'em.

In fact Pete didn't stop here, he went on to tell his teacher in similar detail about aeroplanes and ships. One of the drawbacks to a transcript, as indeed to any kind of printed communication, is that the reader cannot hear the speaker's own voice. In this instance there is such a sense of pent-up energy in Pete's voice on the tape that there is no doubt about his interest in his subject. The talk is unusual in so far as it is in effect really an extended monologue and we shall come back to this use of talk on tape later in the chapter.

What we want to draw attention to above all at this point is the teacher's qualities as a listener. It sounds at the start of the tape as though he is going to interview Pete about dinosaurs and we can imagine the kind of question and answer piece that might easily have resulted. But this doesn't happen – Pete is encouraged by the teacher's attentiveness to tell what he knows without fear of interruption and astonishingly perhaps, out it all comes almost as though he is reading it aloud from behind his eyes.

Occasionally his teacher intervenes when there is a muddle, to help him to sort it out or to make encouraging noises so that he won't founder in the middle of a particularly intractable maze ('That's OK, that's all right, that's fine, fine . . .'). In spite of Pete's limitations as a learner, the teacher has created a situation here in which the pupil is able to regard himself as an expert who can take a justifiable pride in the knowledge that he has acquired. He now knows in addition that he is able to communicate intelligibly to another person, the information that he has been at such pains to gather and this could also be very important to him, both as a means of extending a social relationship and as a means of developing his own identity.

Listening to each other
As teachers ourselves, we are well aware that it is not often possible to devote so much time single mindedly to one student. But increasingly in many schools value is being placed on creating contexts for talk which do not necessarily involve the teacher at all. It is quite common nowadays to find children working in small groups in both science and humanities lessons and in consequence talking more than they would be able to do in a class-taught lesson – and talking more to each other than directly to the teacher.

We would like to consider next three examples of boys talking to their mates, each of which reflects some of the basic motivations for using speech that we outlined at the start of the chapter. In our first piece the teacher is also present, but primarily David is addressing the rest of his class. He was twelve years old at the time and one of the members of a small remedial group in a large comprehensive school. When he arrived at the school a year before, he was unwilling to join in discussions and his writing ability was very limited. However, his teacher discovered that he did many things with his parents – making things, visiting zoos, castles etc – and also that he was a keen observer. So gradually she persuaded him to tell the other children in his group about the things he was interested in. By the time one of our team heard him give this talk about a recent holiday in the Isle of Wight, he had made considerable gains in the confidence with which he addressed the others and in his ability to recreate vividly what he had seen and done so that they could share these remembered experiences with him:

When we was down there was an axe, and we thought it was wax, but it wasn't, it was a real axe, but it was only used once – to kill a person. And when we were looking round there was an automatic machine – the army used to use – but it had two parts missing. And they had the waxworks – men made out of wax – and the trenches with lights flashing on and off like you was really seeing it.

Then I went to Flamingo Park and they had a great big giant lake – and you could buy bags of food – and they were chucking them around and there were loads of them just following me and they were picking food off my feet. You could put your head down; they would just peck food from your hand and they'd just nibble it out of your hand without hurting you at all – it just felt like vibrating – so rough. When I was going round I saw some flamingo birds and I asked the keeper if I could go in and get some pink feathers and that and I went into the ? and got some feathers from there – next time I'll bring some bags of them for you.

And when I was going round – a pigeon. It was on a bench and I had some food and I was just going to give it to a duck when it flew into my hands and we've got that on a film. And my mum says that if Mrs . . . don't mind I can bring the film next week.

David seems to have learned to understand and to forecast the needs of an audience; it is a known audience of peer group and trusted teacher – and the absence of assessment on his audience's part seems to have made David a self-assessor; he can see for himself how well his performance has worked and he can feel a sense of pride and competence from his achievement just as Pete could, telling his teacher about dinosaurs.

Our next piece of talk was sent in to us by a teacher who wrote: 'The situation from which the transcript was taken seems to me notable for the way two very ordinary boys worked together on a simple scientific experiment when left quite alone together to get on with it. For me at any rate it made such a striking contrast between the impression of their abilities gained from the way they worked at the experiment (mutual support, initiative, the talk) and the negative impression gained from their written work in science over the preceding almost three terms.' The boys were two friends in the first-year third stream of a six-form entry school and they were

working from a book by Mee and others called *Science for the 70s*
Experiment 7.2, Unit 7; Electricity:

Here is another way of finding out about charges. You have
four strips of plastic. Two are cellulose acetate (the clear ones),
the others are polystyrene (the opaque ones – the ones you
cannot see through). Rub one of these strips with a duster and
then balance it on the watch glass. Now bring near it a rod of
the same kind which you have rubbed with the same duster,
and observe what happens as you bring the ends near each
other. Do they attract or repel? Each strip has obviously been
given the same charge because they were both treated in
exactly the same way. What do like charges do to each other?
(*Here the book had a diagram.*)

Now repeat the experiment using two strips of the other
material. Do they attract or repel one another? Does this agree
with what you found in the first part of the experiment?

Now rub a strip of one material and balance it on the watch
glass and bring up to it a strip of the other material which you
have also rubbed. What happens this time? Can the charges be
alike? If they are not they must be opposite or 'unlike'. What
can we say that unlike charges do to each other?

This isn't the place to comment on the textbook writers' use of
language, although we think it could be confusing in several places.
Fortunately the boys don't seem to notice as they pay the actual
writing very scant attention!

The teacher who sent it to us wrote: 'The transcript that follows
is as accurate as it could be made (there was some difficulty because
of the noise of handling apparatus), but it cannot convey the
variations in pace and intonation that signalled the changing levels
of interest and excitement.' He notes that five stages in the talk can
be distinguished:

1 setting up the experiment
2 carrying out the first experimental procedures
3 a deviation from the prescribed task – initiating own discoveries

4 the experimenters return to the prescribed task to make a further discovery

5 completion of the worksheets.

Unfortunately we haven't space to print the whole transcript, but here is the passage where the boys deviate from the prescribed task:

G: do your hair
   (Silence)
H: look
   (Silence. The pace of the talk slows as the phenomenon is observed.)
G: it sticks
H: it sticks
G: er it's lifting up
H: I'll try it with this one as well (i.e. the other rod)
   (Silence)
G: rub it again it's maybe not . . . not ready yet
H: here goes . . . here goes
   (Silence)
H: it's lifting it up
G: is it . . . out of the way . . . I'll try it (Silence) yeh (Silence) it's rising a little
H: it does the same to your hairs dun it . . . it makes your hairs rise
G: yeh
H: you can feel it the electricity
G: yeh it must be in the electricity
   (Silence)
H: let's try this one
   (One of the experimenters is rubbing one of the strips)
G: out of the way . . . out of the way quickly (Short inaudible utterances) it doesn't make much difference the electricity (Silence) crumbs
H: I like the way it lifts it up
G: it doesn't lift it up very much but it lifts it up (Silence) oh look
H: they attract don't they

G and H: yeh

G: it must be the electricity from the . . . (inaudible – listening to the tape, the speaker couldn't tell what he said either)

H: it lifts up your hairs as well

G: put it on your head (inaudible) all right put it on your head (Silence)
it lifts up your hairs as well (Reading from text) What do like charges do to each other?
(Listening to the tape H thinks he said 'light' charges. He can't believe he said 'like' because it doesn't make sense to him.)

H: lifts them up don't they

G: yeh . . . hold it let's try it the other way round . . . here I'll rub this one . . . put it on here . . . out of the way quickly

H: let's see if it works the other way round

G: right . . . that's right . . . two strips of the other

H: wait there I want to see if it works the other way round (Silence)

H: it don't work so good . . . this one's too light

G: it does

H: does it

G: yes that's the same kind in it

H: look at that (They discover the strip will lift paper)

G: crumbs

H: look at that lift the paper up

G: crumbs

H: it attract dun it

G: yes . . . crumbs look . . . it lifted that paper up crumbs . . . it's excellent that isn't it
(Silence) it's lifting that rod up can you see it (Silence)

H: you can feel it rise . . . what one's that (Silence)

G: that that one right then . . . yes try . . . (The reference is to the first prescribed experiment.)

H: let's do that one again anyway . . . right

G: do it the other way round this time

The talk makes two things clear: the boys understand at this stage little more (if anything!) about electricity than they did at the start of the experiment, but they are interested, their curiosity has been roused sufficiently to prompt them to try out one or two possibilities of their own – 'Do your hair' and 'Let's try this one' etc. They are pleased with their observations and quite unaware that they are not following the same controls or procedures that they were directed to follow in the book; for them the satisfaction is derived from seeing things happen: 'I like the way it lifts up' and 'Crumbs!'. They pick up, even if only briefly, the spirit (if not the method) of scientific experiment as we can tell from such comments as 'Let's see if it works the other way round.' Their discovery that the strip will actually lift paper sparks off real excitement – enough to motivate them to *redo* the original experiment. All in all a promising learning situation.

Our third example of boys using talk together in a group illustrates how they can collaborate with each other to make something in words – just for fun. They are having a go here at doing a Monty Python Silly Sketch of their own. We quote just the first couple of minutes from their final version on tape although in fact they worked at this and two other sketches with a fair amount of commitment (and a good deal of hilarity) for two double periods. Readers will have to do their best to imagine the silly voices.

Announcer: Human relations, part one, sex education. This – play – includes – two judges, three doctors, one lollipop lady plus (very fast) four supporting kinky people. The spectacular takes place in a (?) somewhere in England. By the way it would be of great interest to the listeners (interjection) – Sydney is wondering why I said two judges, three doctors, one lollipop lady when they're not in any way necessary to the story. In fact I think I've lost my sanity. (Voice off: True!) Well, never mind, I'll find it later.

New voice: Ah – well, ladies and gentlemen, sex education has always been described as taking a child who appears to be totally ignorant of sex aside at a certain age and turning it into a randy little . . . who can't be let out of sight. Well, this is completely wrong because they believe in giving it 'it' in an 'ilarious talk that lasts about three and a half minutes. This so-called 'ilarious talk is either given by a parent or a geography teacher who both seem to take this particular subject seriously – which to most young sods spoils the whole fun of learning what they have done by about the age of eight was a mistake.

Toffee-nosed voice: This of course is simply nonsense.

Another voice: I wanted to say that (sniff sniff) I wanted to say that (tearfully with mounting distress) that's the only bit I wanted to say!

Another voice: These bleedin' quacks are quacking up. (Uproar)

Announcer: Translated, that means 'You're all mad – quite mad.'

Various: We're not – we're not.

Announcer: You are. (In harmony, but very unmelodiously on a rising scale.)

Various: We're not – we're not – we're not.

Announcer: You are – you are – you are.

Voice: If that's singing harmony I'm a duck's uncle.

Another interesting use of talk in school, which may or may not involve the teacher as a participant but avoids the dominant structuring of the class-taught lesson, is when a group work together to improvise imaginatively round a particular situation. Unfortunately, as most of our collected work from schools has been writing, we have no tape at hand to illustrate how effectively this kind of dramatic involvement can engage the whole group and how rapidly the talk can become exploratory in an effort to predict how the behaviour of each individual will affect what happens next: Will the African tribe accept that the missionary brings the truth about God with him? Will they become divided amongst themselves? How will they react to a conflict which strikes at the roots of their present beliefs and practices? Or – how would a French aristocrat feel and behave when faced by a hostile Parisian mob? What would he say and how would they respond? These are both improvisations that we have seen involving children speculatively – and sometimes passionately – in talk.

Taped talk

On those particular occasions we did not happen to have a tape recorder handy so now we are only able to recollect what happened in a fairly general sort of way – which brings us to our next point in this chapter – the tremendous usefulness of taped talk. In many ways the invention of tape recorders has provided us with a medium of expression which retains all the advantages of talk whilst adding some of the advantages which traditionally have belonged to writing. Tape can be kept, it can be listened to any number of times, it can be transcribed, discussed, even redrafted and revised. All the examples of talk that we have quoted so far would have been unquotable without the help of a tape recorder. We know that since *Language, the Learner and the School* was published in the late 1960s many teachers have developed insights into how talk can be used through listening to similar tapes made in their own classrooms and the classrooms of colleagues. It has been possible to study in detail how groups of children learn from talking to each other without a teacher present once they become used to discussing round a tape recorder. Teachers who have been able to use taping extensively in this way will know how quickly pupils can come to accept such recordings without any sense that what they say will be 'used as evidence against them' later. Often they are eager to play back their discussions, plays or whatever to the teacher themselves.

A history teacher who has worked with us was pleasantly surprised when he used tape recorders for the first time with a third year class to find that many pupils were keen to revise the plays they had made after they had listened to their first efforts on tape. He commented that where there would have been groans all round if he had suggested that they redraft any written work, in this instance suggestions for improving what they had done came from them.

We also know of some sixth formers who have discussed one of their own previous discussions with keen interest from a transcript typed out for them by the teacher. The teacher had handed out copies of the transcript without telling the group what it was. Gradually the fact that it was *their own talk* that they were reading dawned on them and a further interesting discussion about the differences between spoken and written language took place (subsequently also transcribed by the teacher for them and for us!). We mention this not so much because the subject of their second discussion was about these language differences, but because it indicates how valuable it can be to preserve talk so that it can be talked about further.

Another potentially valuable use of tape as an alternative to writing is when a pupil uses it to voice his thoughts out loud about something. The 'something' could be what he remembers and thinks and feels about some part of his own past experience, or it could be speculation, or it could be an effort to tell what he knows, rather like Pete telling his teacher about dinosaurs. Finding ways of reshaping and reformulating new information is often a problem for the learner and talk can provide an excellent starting point, especially if what is said can then be heard again and considered further.

One of the most interesting pieces of 'extended monologue' of this kind which has been examined by us in detail in *From Information to Understanding* comes from a tape recording that Trevor, a first-year boy, made in preparation for a talk to his class about the evolution of man. In this first attempt of his to put it together, we have been able to trace how he learns more by having to search for a shape for what he wants to say. In the struggle to do this, he perceives the significance of what he has read and heard *as he goes along* and on the tape it is possible to hear his mounting excitement as these discoveries dawn on him.

Coincidentally we later came across another boy in the first year at another school who had also been working on the topic of 'Early Man' and at the suggestion of his teacher was able to use taped talk to shape what he already 'knew' and to add to it. Andrew had been given a worksheet which gave some information about the trapping of animals. He had then done three drawings of primitive traps. He offered to write about these but in fact was only able to

write a couple of lines which neither he nor his teacher could read –
at which point the teacher suggested that he should talk about them
on tape. A brief discussion followed about what Andrew might say –
that he could for instance describe the traps and how they were used.
These suggestions are taken up at considerable length and with
evident enthusiasm. It is quite clear from the transcript that
Andrew did in fact know a fair amount about the various devices
used for trapping animals. He said afterwards that the pictures he
had drawn were vividly in his mind. Once his concentration has
been shifted from the act of writing (which he still can't manage
easily), to the information inside his head, he can produce far more
than his initial two lines might have suggested. In practical terms
he is more at home with talk, as it is quicker and allows for quali-
fications as he goes along in a way that writing often doesn't. It also
seems that through his re-creation of these hunting scenes in words,
he can begin to capture the feelings that the men experienced –
excitement, satisfaction, frustration, exhaustion.

Just as Trevor discovers more about man's evolution by shaping
what he knows in speech, so here Andrew discovers more than he
consciously knew already by talking about it to the tape recorder –
and beyond that, to his teacher. We think that the awareness of
feeling which he generated in his description of how men trapped
animals (e.g. 'they used to creep along until they see an animal and
then they used to spread out silently', 'some get tired and men die')
was responsible finally for the story *Animal's Death* which adds a
different dimension to the earlier account of what actually happened.
Again we know from what Andrew said afterwards that he made the
story up as he went along. We quote the whole tape:

The title is called *Animals, Animals Die – Death*. A long time
ago people and men used to live, used to live in kind of jungle
time, but if they wanted to live they had to catch animals and
things like that. But it was hard so they had to build traps. They
would build a trap and dig (and everything?) They'd use wood,
and sticks, sticks and bones and things to dig holes. And they
used to catch them with, with sticks and spears and things like
that. They used to go in a hunting group. They used to creep
along until they see an animal and then they used to spread out

silently. They were spreading to make him go to the way of the trap and then they would all shoot out and scare him. The animal would run and go straight to the trap. There would be spears and pieces like that in the trap – they didn't like doing this but they had to – this was how they had to stay alive. After they had caught the animal – it depended what kind of animal it was – they would take it back. They would split it up between the hunting men and then spread a ring (?). One of the hunting men would get two sticks, make a hole in one of the sticks and rub them together to make fire. This is how they did it: they rubbed and rubbed until smoke would come; all of a sudden it would catch alight; they used to put it under a, some straw and things like that, then they used to put the animal on a stick, the stick going right along his body. They would turn it and whirl it to make it burn. The womens would just watch it while the men went hunting again to look for more. After they had caught one animal they would go looking for more. As you know they'd build all kinds of traps. There was an elephant trap when they'd get a piece of string and put it along two pieces of tree and put, add it to a piece of wood, a pointed point – piece – hanging from the tree, and as the elephant would walk across it it would fall and go straight into the elephant. When the men would find it they would not know how to carry it. It sometimes, it takes a long while, they had to take it in days. They split up into little groups to pull it each day. Some get tired because they do not have transport things like we do these days. As you know it is so hard. They get tired and men die. They get bugs, they get fevers, they get all kinds of things. Some die with poison. Some of them go fishing and get food like that, but the fish is not big enough for them, they need more and more. Sometimes it's hard to get water. It is very hard. I, I am glad I am not one of them so I wish you were not. If you find out some about this it is very good, it is a very good project, things like this. There is another sort of trap but this trap, a man must stay there all the time, he carries a knife around with him. He sits and waits until one animal would go under a tree. At the top of that tree there would be a net and bushes and things, they would be heavy. That net would have a piece of string attaching to it, coming down from behind a tree and tied to the floor by a peg or something. When the bloke see an animal underneath it he would cut the rope, all of a sudden the net would just fly under. Then the bloke would go and kill it, chop it up and take it, take it back to the camp. They would all spread round and look and see if it was a good catch. Sometimes they get more if they catch them but I do not know, so, I don't know, I can't tell you.

That is all I can tell you about catching animals, but now I'm going to tell you a story called *Animal's Death*.

A long time ago there was a chief of a camp, and he had a pet animal called Shiva, and Shiva, Shiva lived out in the jungle but sometimes he'd be in trouble and get caught, but sometimes he got out of it by, by the, that, that captain of that group. He would tell, tell his men to leave it alone and let it free but sometimes it, it was too late. So one, once upon a time Shiva went, went alone – he was not married and didn't have no cubs – he liked being alone. As he walked through jungles and things like that he got tired too because he could not find water, but he never knew where he could go or where he could live because the hunting men were always out hunting for the people. Sometimes they, they would hunt in lots of groups, sometimes they would split up, but always three or four in a group. Shiva would walk miles and miles and miles, sometimes he would walk alone, sometimes he would hide in the bushes, behind rocks. The men, when the men see him, they used to throw spears, stones and things at him, but somehow Shiva escaped from the lot of them. He dug tunnels and found caves, lived in them and got shelter. He would hide in caves and get away from the rains and storms and things. But sometimes his friends, Shiva's friends, they got hurt badly, he didn't really know what to do about them. He's not a human and he's not, not really capable to talk. The only thing he can do is kill, eat and, and live. He sometimes feels ill, sometimes nearly dies, but it's occasional. Sometimes he finds special medicines, sometimes his favourite chief helps him out. He has a way of speaking to his chief and a way he can get away. But one, one day he was walking alone, somehow the men must have known he was coming this way. They all spreaded out behind the bushes. There was a trap in the middle of the bush, and as, as he was coming up to the trap they all scared him. Shiva ran, ran, ran, ran – ran as fast as he could. He did not know what to do and as he got closer and closer to the trap he got scared and scared. He carried on running. As he jumped for a man he landed straight in a trap. There was all spears and things at the bottom of the trap, they killed him, it killed him dead – no signs of life again. The chief was so angry he put all the men to death and that was all I know about them. The men died, they died with, with hunger and thirst. The chief was so unhappy he died, he died from unhappiness. His wife was so sorry that she killed herself because all the men had been so horrible killing Shiva when the chief had told them not to, she had to. And all the people after that were so unhappy and never, never will kill another animal called Shiva again.

There is one further use of taped talk that we would like to look at briefly because in several ways it has interesting links with writing. We are referring to that increasingly widespread (and popular) activity in 'integrated studies' or 'project' work called interviewing. Armed with cassettes, singly or in small groups, students escape from school for an hour or two and invade the local neighbourhood. The aim is to collect information from real people about this topic or that which can then be fed back into their school-based studies. This means that, like so much writing in school, the purpose of the talk is predominantly transactional – to relay information. What often happens in many such interviews is exactly what happens very often in children's transactional writing – the speaker or writer feels constrained to give us the facts impersonally, from the point of view of an impassive outsider who has nothing 'to do' with the information that is being related. In both cases we are presented with half a picture or perhaps more appositely, with a picture in black and white. Undeniably one function of an interview is to obtain information, but its other function is to reflect the thoughts and feelings of the person being interviewed – it is his interpretation of the facts that gives such information its full meaning and significance.

We want you, if you will, to compare what happens in two different interviews. Both come from an educational project investigating 'a sense of audience'. (This project was conducted in the summer term 1974 by John Foggin and Chris Noble, then at Northern Counties College of Education and Jill Beaumont, then at Sandhurst School.) A first-year class from a Newcastle comprehensive school exchanged materials (tapes, slides, photographs, writing) on the topic 'Where We Live' with a similar class from Sandhurst. Both groups as part of the project decided to interview old people in each town to find out what memories they had of living there in the past.

For our purposes here, the two interviews that we have picked out illustrate clearly the differences between transactional and expressive talk. Steven (s) takes his role as an interviewer seriously – he has prepared beforehand the questions that he wants to ask. This sense that there is a job to be done, enhanced no doubt by the tape recorder and the microphone, communicates itself to his grandmother (G) who conscientiously sticks to the facts and makes an effort to phrase them in appropriately formal language:

S: What did you do for a living?

G: I always wanted to be a nurse and went to the Northern General Hospital, Lincoln, training for three years. Then you went into a military hospital there for two years. My wages were one pound and ten pennies a month.

S: What did your husband do for a living?

G: My husband was a tram driver. His wages were two pounds and ten pence a week. His hobbies were gardening and bowls.

S: What do you think of the changes in Newcastle, for instance the Byker Wall? What do you think of that and the new houses around it?

G: There are many changes taking place in Newcastle and some buildings (which?) are now being built and the Byker Wall gives a very bad impression. They look just like pigeon crees. But when one enters these flats you get a different impression. They are simply lovely, warm and cosy, and have all modern conveniences. They have a sound barrier to prevent the noise of the buses passing through them. They accommodate about 300 people.

We can hear from the tape how absolutely Steven was tied to the questions he had prepared and because he is concentrating so hard on the questions he wants to ask he can't really listen to his grandmother or enjoy what she says or respond to the content of her talk – very like a new teacher who holds to his lesson plan regardless of student response. Steven's teacher was understandably disappointed with the brevity and the rather stilted tone of the interview, especially as Steven had told the group before he made the recording what a talker his grandmother was and entertained them with an archetypal leg anecdote that was obviously a favourite of hers:

S: Me granma . . . eh, she's seventy-eight I think . . . she used to be a nurse during the war.

T: Did she? That should be very interesting. (Brief bit of general talk omitted.)

S: Yes, she talks on for ages and ages.

T: Sounds just what we want then.

S: One of the stories she told was when she was working in the RVI and this lady had had her leg amputated and they had taken it away to another hospital to say what was wrong with it you know, examine it, and the man . . . I don't know what he was, he had to take it and he didn't know it was a leg in it and it dropped out of the parcel thing . . . and it was in the street . . .

T: Did he just think it was a package or something like that?

S: Yeh, that he had to deliver and he didn't know it was a leg. (Laughter)

T: . . . what else did she do? Was she a housewife after that?

S: Yeh.

T: Whereabouts did she live?

S: She lives over on Heaton.

T: Has she always lived there?

S: Just about, yes.

T: . . . so she'll have seen a lot of changes living down there.

Certainly, when we come to the interview there is a strong sense that a splendid opportunity to draw all sorts of information from his grandmother about these changes has been missed because Steven made the mistake of overstructuring his approach.

Tim and Kev, the two Sandhurst boys, took their interviewing seriously too. They decorated the cover of the transcript with a carefully coloured-in drawing of a proscenium arch inscribed with the words 'This tape was directed and produced by Tim Morton and Kev Ibbotson.' They were fortunate because when they reached the house where they were to tape the interview, a friend of the old lady who lived there happened to call in. The result is that the two of them keep each other talking in a relaxed and gossipy sort of way. Where Steven's grandmother had to slot her replies into the framework of his questions, these two pick up on each other's memories and comments. Consequently their talk is much more expressive – it is also both more entertaining and more informative. We quote about half the transcript the boys made (as they wrote it); significantly it is much longer than our first example:

OF is the 'old friend' of one or both the boys presumably.
OL is the 'old lady' who called in.

OF: You can't stay long I'm busy. thease boys want to know how sandhurst has altered, how many years?

  T: O it doesn't matter.

OL: O a lot, heaps. (mumble) o a long away, for one thing the first big improvement was to make this big road as there was no road.

OF: And no street lights. Now what date was that, When you come?

OL: When we come was the year (mumble) you can reckon up can't you. (Silence) 1917.

OF: There was no street lights, well that – you could put that down can't you.

OL: And there was –

OF: What's that then.

OL: No road outside.

OF: oh your talking, oh alright.

  K: Its a tape recorder.

OF: Oh yea.

OL: Outside was only gravel.

OF: There was no paving no path.

OL: No proper path.

OF: And no er Kerbs, yea see.

 T: Just gravel.

OF: mm

OL: And over the road opposite there where those houses are that was two haystacks.

OF: And fields.

OL: And all fields.

OF: And er each side of the road was ditches you know what I mean by ditches don't you, yes.

OL: Do you like (look?) outside ere – else there was a long ditch from there

OF: That wall

OL: To ere.

OF: You know the wall outside.

OL: The hedges over there used to be a former ditch.

OF: mm

OL: And over the road where the pillar box is, is the pillar box still over there?

OF: No that been er moved

OL: That was a ditch and whats more more to – to satisfy you that was a ditch and the sweep the name rollins he was

OF: That used to be here

OL: he had a daughter that daughter fell in that ditch and broke her leg and had to have her leg cut off and the girls still alive over there

OF: Lives over there now mm

OL: Yes, oh there ton's of alterations now.

OF: Yea,

 T: um

OF: What else, what else is there we can say, what

 T: Er has transport and things like that changed noticably at all

OF: O yes, you mean buses now.

 T: Yes

OF: Yes, well when first we come there was only a bus used to run every three

OL: About twice a day a funny old thing

OF: Yea

OL: Like a coach

OF: From here to, only from er

OL: Here to Crowthorne

OF: From Camberly

OL: Marleys little girl had cut her finger off and

OF: Well we don't want all that.

OL: Showed the thing to go didn't we

OF: mm yes, it only used to run from Sandhurst to Crowthorne every bit three hours.

K: No long bus services etc

OF: No what

K: No er ones from say here to er Camberley something like that.

OF: Yes from here to Camberley and Crowthorne but not to Reading.

OL: This man had

K: I see

OL: his own

OF: No no

OL: bus and used to run it.

T: Do you think the polution has encreased at all in recent years

OF: What, you mean the population of the people?

T: No the polution of um the air

OF: Polution er whats polution now you see I'm a silly, what do you call polution?

K: er

OL: Rotern water, stinking

K: Yea

T: Yes

OL: Yes yes

OF: O yes thats improved, yes that's improved a big improvement that is.

OL: A lot has improved and a lot hasn't

K: mm

OL: And a lot hasn't, there's this ditch still along there and there used to be a ditch that ran along the bottom of this garden along there

OF: And we don't get the floods like we used to

OL: And what more Ill tell you something else. There was no water closet there was no proper WC

OF: Well you wouldn't know that would you

OL: No but you could put it in the tape recorder

OF: Earth bucket what do you call earth bucket

OL: There was no WC it was a bucket and the man used to come round twice a week and he would empty it for 9d There was two houses we had next door and this, my Mother and Father there and me ere. Well this man used to come and I think he was half tight to take your pail of er anything away and im being drunk he stopped it and my father used to carry on and said we can't stick this he said this mess all along the road so the consequence was we had to have a hole down the garden to go and empty it.

OF: mm er well they wouldnt remember that.

From talking to writing

At the beginning of this chapter we noted how most children have already learnt to use talking for a variety of purposes before they even come to school. Unfortunately we cannot say that just as many learn to use writing for similar reasons, even after ten to eleven years of compulsory 'education'. We want to make two suggestions:

1 Writing which is much closer to talk than most school writing is at present should be encouraged right through the child's years at school – and across the whole curriculum. We believe that such writing would free the writer to think in writing and to learn through using written language in the same way that he already uses talk.

2 Writing should be used for a much wider range of purposes in school than 'just testing' – in fact for much the same purposes that talk is used for quite spontaneously by children to answer their needs and to further their development. We believe that it would be much easier to interrelate talk and writing in the learning process if both served these same purposes in school in all subjects.

Both these suggestions have important implications for the audience to whom the talk or the writing is addressed. We have seen how children can use talk to learn from each other in a variety of situations – and how the teacher who is willing to listen with real interest and attention to his pupils is able to help them to learn through their own talk. We note with interest that where the audience in Steven's interview with his grandmother came closest to our category of examiner, in a question and answer situation, the talk froze and conveyed less than it could have done.

We have also seen how the introduction of tape recording as another form of communication has extended, often excitingly, the ways in which talk can be used to further learning – and how it can often help to interrelate talking and writing for children of all abilities.

In the rest of this book we try to show how writing can in fact be used for the same purposes as talk in ways that can enrich learning opportunities in all subjects. We also try to show how the development of writing in both the transactional and poetic functions *depends* on the writer keeping his own voice to shape what is new in relation to what he already knows. We hope that our excursion into talk in this chapter will help to point the way to more productive ways of working in schools with written language too.

References

BARNES, D. (1969) 'Language in the secondary classroom' in D. Barnes, J. Britton and H. Rosen *Language, the Learner and the School* Penguin

BRITTON, J. (1970) *Language and Learning* Penguin

MEE, A.J., BOYD, P. and RITCHIE, D. (1972) *Science for the 70s* Heinemann Educational

WEIR, R. (1962) *Language in the Crib* The Hague: Mouton

WRITING ACROSS THE CURRICULUM PROJECT *From Information to Understanding* Ward Lock Educational

Chapter three

Making sense of new information

Feedback to the teacher

We have already described in chapter one how in the original writing research sample, the bulk of the writing done in secondary schools was concerned with information. On the whole, the function of this writing seemed to be reporting back by pupils mostly in a generalised way on what they had been told, or read in books. We noted how writing was often being used, apparently more for the teachers' purposes than the pupils' – to demonstrate what knowledge had been acquired rather than to help the process of converting unfamiliar information into new knowledge. We noted how in almost every subject writing was concerned in this way with learning *that had already happened*, where a priority was placed on clarity and precision both of expression and organisation. Sometimes just 'the facts' were recorded: natural resources, chief imports and exports, seed dispersal, the human reproductive system (with diagram), life in Tudor England (with drawings). In the 4th and 5th years reasons were added but more often supplied by the teacher than suggested by the pupils. The research team's impression was that much of what was being written down had no inherent interest for the writer; it was not being put to use by him in any way other than to prove that he had 'done his homework'.

We expect you are already familiar with the kind of writing we are describing but to refresh your memory here are two fairly typical pieces; both were regarded by the teacher as worth a high mark. The point we want to make is not however an evaluative one, it is concerned more with analysis than evaluation: what is happening in each piece for the writer? Are there any hints that new learning has taken place? For what audience is the student writing? Is he or she making a genuine communication or a spurious one? Is there any sense of commitment to what is being written down – any enthusiasm or interest which conveys itself to the reader?

The first piece is taken from a second year girl's project on lighthouses and the other from a fifth year girl's history notebook (different schools):

How lights developed   Jane (11–12)

For hundreds of years, fires in 'chauffers' were the main beacons of Northern Europe. There was one at Tynemouth Castle as early as 1540 and there was one still in use at St Bees, Cumberland in 1822.

Open fires gave a good blaze to penetrate the gloom of murky nights, but they used enormous amounts of wood and coal.

Candles, long popular in the clearer air of Italy, were used in the first three Eddystone lighthouses. Smeaton arranged twenty four huge candles in two circles, but in 1810 the light was converted to oil. Whiteside used oil for his smalls (?) light. Candles and oil lamps had to be screened from wind and rain, but windows quickly became black with soot. In 1784 the problem was solved. Ami Argaud, a Swiss, invented a smokeless lamp made of two thin, brass tubes, one inside the other, with a circular wick between. He accidentally improved it when he found that the neck of a broken flask placed on top would draw up the flame and make it burn brilliantly. After this glass chimnies were always added. Argaud lamps are widely used for lighting homes, and made possible great developments in lighthouse lights.

Josiah Wedgwood 1730-95   Clare (15–16)

Josiah Wedgwood was born in north Staffordshire. He was the 13th son of a master potter. He began work in the family pottery business at the age of 9 years old and was self educated. When he was twelve he contracted small pox, which as a result caused him to have a leg amputated in later life.

The pottery industry was already well-established in Staffordshire where there was plenty of clay and coal. However, the pottery produced there was of poor design and texture. Josiah Wedgwood saw possibilities for expansion. Roads and canals allowed easier transport of heavy commodities such as coal and clay since they had been improved, and also allowed safer transit of fragile pottery.

The 18th century saw a rise in population and an increase in the standard of living. Tea, chocolate and coffee drinking, already popular with the rich, was becoming the poorer people's habit. The rich wanted high quality ware, while the rest of the population sought less expensive sets of pottery. Plate was expensive, pewter was scarce, porcelain too fragile.

Wedgwood's pottery was to supply the needs of all tastes. His success was due to the quality of his produce, his original designs, the specialisation of labour, and his sales organisation. Wedgwood established a new factory at Etruria, near Burslem, in 1769. There using the new discoveries of green glaze, cream-ware and jasper-ware he produced quality goods for the rich. He soon won world fame. The most famous were the elegant vases with a white decoration on the 'wedgwood blue' back-grounds. As Italian or classical motifs were in vogue, he employed the great designer, Flatman. Wedgwood used the heads of Popes for goods sold in Spain, Italy and South America. He had a display room at Etruria and in 1765 opened a showroom in London.

Wedgwood was a perfectionist. He used to walk around the factory smashing with his stick any piece which was sub-standard and chalked onto the bench. 'This won't do for Josiah Wedgwood.' His workers responded well. He increased production by a division of labour. Instead of one man performing every process, Wedgwood employed specialists – some mixed clay, others worked on the potter's wheel, some did the firing and some the glazing.

Sales were increased. In order to cater for the popular taste the 'willow pattern' was produced. Advertisements appeared in newspapers, discounts were given and catalogues appeared translated in Europe. In his time Wedgwood was called 'Vase Maker General to the Universe'. Josiah Wedgwood died in 1795 worth £500,000.

Now consider our questions: first, what is happening in each piece of writing for the writer? What Jane has written sounds as though it is taken largely from someone else's writing (i.e. from a book) and what Clare has written is based on notes taken down in class from the teacher, with reference also, possibly, to a history text-book. Neither piece is coloured by the writer's own voice. It may be of course that both girls were interested in the subject they were writing about, but because neither offers any comments of her own about the information that is being recorded, there doesn't appear to be any consideration of the facts or any attempt to interpret their significance. Neither was there any writing in Jane's project, or in Claire's notebook, either before or after these pieces which would suggest that they were part of an ongoing process of learning.

So what was the purpose of the writing and who was it for? The two questions are interrelated. In our view, as is so often the case in school, the writing was for the teacher because it had been set as a task; it provides the teacher with evidence that Jane had done some reading and that Claire now has her own potted biography of Wedgwood's life. That seems to be all. We have no idea whether Claire asked herself any questions – about Wedgwood's business methods, for instance, or whether his employees enjoyed working for him; and in Jane's case, whether she really understood what Argaud's lamp was like ┬ how it functioned and how he came to make his discovery. There is no sense here that a response is being made to the information that is set down. It seems to be kept at arm's length as if the writer is viewing it from a distance, instead of coming up close to examine it in detail.

Reconstruction or reproduction?

Is education really about taking on a received body of knowledge in this way? How much of the information that children are presented with in school becomes a permanent part of their view of the world? How much of it affects their lives in any way apart from providing some of them with a handful of examination passes? Perhaps there are other ways of learning about the world they live in which can be more valuable or useful. If we look into our own experiences, how do we gain insights or perceive truths which are of real significance to us? Surely they emerge gradually from our own continual reconstruction of reality as it is modified or extended from day to day by what we do or say or hear or see or read. Of course we learn from each other, but in order to do so effectively each of us has to remain at the centre of our own learning.

There is an illuminating comment in the fourth chapter of the Bullock Report (DES 1975) which describes the problem clearly:

> It is a confusion of everyday thought that we tend to regard 'knowledge' as something that exists independently of someone who knows. 'What is known' must in fact be brought to life afresh in every 'knower' by his own efforts. . . . In order to accept what is offered when we are told something, we have to have somewhere to put it; and having somewhere to put it means that the framework of past knowledge and experience into which it must fit is adequate as a means of interpreting and apprehending it. Something approximating to finding out for ourselves needs therefore to take place if we are to be successfully told.

The discoveries, concerns and interests of others can be shared by the learner if he so chooses – and if he sees the point; they cannot be imposed.

To start from the child's own needs and interests is not of course a new idea for teachers – but at secondary level in England it seems remarkably difficult to implement, partly as the result of our present system of external examinations. Currently students in secondary schools, particularly in the 4th and 5th years, are required to do the same experiments, read the same books and write down the same facts – more or less. Moreover, the perspectives from which they are expected to handle information are often narrow in so far as the concern of the teacher is more often with 'getting it right' than with looking for avenues of individual interest. We know that examiners are adjured to give marks for original thinking, but when it comes to the crunch, the ticks mostly go to the points which they already have in mind, (sometimes even printed on the official mark-sheet in front of them) and for which they scan each paper as they make their way through the pile of scripts.

In the Development Project we have been looking among other things for writing in which the pupil was in some way personally engaged and in this chapter we would like to present some of the pieces we have come across which have a strong informational element but in which something more seems to be happening than simple playback to the teacher. Many of our pieces are from children aged eleven to thirteen, partly because the first three years of our work were mainly concerned with this age group – and partly because we have found a greater freedom for a variety of approaches to learning and a greater willingness to experiment in the first two or three years of secondary schooling.

Some of the writing is technically inaccurate, produced with a struggle by children who are shaky on how to manage the code of written language. But we have been looking not so much for an ability to spell and punctuate correctly as for signs of a different kind of engagement with the work in hand.

There are many ways in which we can set about making sense of new information. Every day we reconstrue our experiences as we remember, reflect, select, connect, imagine, speculate; we can also (and this is where writing perhaps can be most useful), do the more complex job of organising our memories, reflections, selections, connections, imaginings and speculations. In turn these reconstructions of experience provide us with fresh insights and perceptions. Again, if we check back to our own experience, colouring all these activities is some kind of feeling which drives us on: it may be a strong sense of curiosity or excitement, of enjoyment or sheer determination. But unless we experience some positive feeling, the facts will never be galvanised into life for us solely because we are required to write about them.

Mostly of course, what is new information for one individual, is already 'knowledge' for many others. But 'What is known must be brought to life afresh in every knower'; unless we are given the opportunity to reconstrue and to assimilate gradually what is new, for us the information will remain inert, a scatter of facts which have no real significance because they have not taken shape within our own consciousness.

We believe that often examinations do not value sufficiently this kind of learning by gradual reconstruction. It is quite possible for candidates to impress examiners by reproducing what they have been told accurately and in detail. Revising for an exam still involves memorising notes, quotations, diagrams and dates just long enough for them all to be poured out onto paper in their appropriate sequence under the correct subheadings. Many of us have passed examinations quite successfully in this way, especially if we happened to be speedy handwriters. But information that can be forgotten within a matter of weeks (days sometimes) cannot be counted as 'knowledge'. Without a much more fundamental grasp of the facts than short-term memorising allows for, none of us will reach the point where we can make original perceptions of our own – however many examiners we manage to impress.

Perhaps writing for an examiner audience always has an element of constriction about it – of showing that you know what they expect you to know. It is at any rate interesting to notice that many of the pieces that follow do not appear to be written for such an audience. In every case where a sense of positive engagement with the facts occurs, the writer has something as well as the information to offer (his own experience, his own thoughts, his own feelings or observations), *which is not already known* to the teacher or the wider audience for whom he is writing.

At the centre of their own learning

Debbie chose to do a project in her second year on bird watching, partly she said because she knew a bit about birds already and partly because she preferred doing work out of school to work from books. Here is the first entry of the diary Debbie kept of her weekly outings over several weeks with John G. a student teacher. Basically it is a record of what she remembers seeing but there is a sense of pleasure in the act of recapturing what she saw and heard which motivates her to set down her pictures of each bird as clearly as possible, not by copying a standard description from a book but by finding her own words. The writing is expressive, moving towards the transactional function because Debbie is keen to inform us about what she saw.

Bird watching   Debbie (12–13)
Before we got to the Railway we heard a robin then another came and in the end there were three. Then we came to twelve blackbirds on a football field and also a song thrush feeding. Next we saw about 5 black headed gulls in fact they are the

smallest gulls in britain in summer they have a chocolatey head and in winter they have a white head with a black spot behind the eye then we saw a bluetit flying towards us then on the other side of the road we saw a great tit. The great tits have like a black cap and beard which goes in between its legs up to its tail and has white cheeks and a yellow waistcoat and brown wings and a brown tail then suddenly we saw a small brown bird with like a stub as a tail it was a wren then we saw a blackbird's nest with inter twining twigs, feathers leaves then overhead we saw two wood pigeons fly over then we saw a chaffinch female she had a brown body with a black tail with white feathers at each side. Next we saw a hedge sparrow it was brown and very dark brown in stripes next we saw a crow's nest and some common lapwings which are green on top of the body and white underneath.

Keeping their own diary entries seems to work well for many children. Here are some excerpts from *The Diary of a Blackbird* which was written by a fourth year boy over a period of several weeks during the summer term. It begins with a list of questions that he wanted to find out about, then his observations follow, after which he is able to answer the questions he started with.

Blackbird behaviour   Tim (14–15)

These are the questions I want to answer.

1 Territorial boundaries
  (Make a map positioning territory)
2 The food diet
3 His favourite singing posts
4 Does his song differ from the other blackbirds?
5 Which bird incubates the eggs?
6 Behaviour of the male towards the female
7 Behaviour of male towards other females
8 How does the male defend his territory
9 Are there special feeding times
10 Does the male have any special singing times.

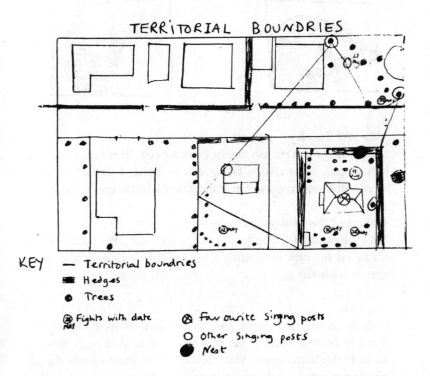

TERRITORIAL BOUNDRIES

KEY
— Territorial boundries
▰ Hedges
● Trees
⊗ Fights with date   ⊗ Favourite singing posts
MAY   O Other Singing posts
                      ● Nest

May 20th Monday 12 noon
Male blackbird is singing in the ashtree to the south of the
house. After about 5 minutes he flew to the scots pine in the
front garden. His song is deepish and musical he sings in bursts
of song each around fifteen seconds long. first brood has left
the nest.

12.15 pm
Male blackbirds down the road start to sing the blackbird I am
studing stops singing.

1.15 pm
Male blackbird feeding in garden on a few berries and worms. I
have found a way to distinguish him from other blackbirds. He
has a thin white streak down his back and has got a white patch
on his left wing. He has also a white patch around his right eye.

May 21st Tuesday   4.15 pm
Male is singing in the ash tree he is facing east. Every time I see him singing he is always facing east or north I think this is because the most arggesive male blackbird is in the north or east.

May 22nd Wednesday   9.00 am
Male blackbird feeding two young ones, while the female is sitting on the nest incubating a second clutch consisting of 3 eggs. it is usually 4.

12.45 pm
Male is on the next doors roof he has just stopped singing. Another Male blackbird has flew up to him. first male flew down to the lawn second Male followed they fluttered into the air, clawing at each other with feet and pecking with their bills, after that they flew off in different directions.

May 25th Saturday   10 am
The male sees another female he flies up to it and he chases her over the cornfield.

11.15 am
Male chase song thrush over cornfield for no apprent reason.

12.15 pm
Male singing on the roof he is facing north. This is his favourite singing post probably because intruders can see him clearly and be warned.

May 27th Monday
Male has been in two fights he has suffered feather loss he's got

a bald patch on his back but is still singing strongly the fights were on the east borders of his territory.

May 28th Tuesday   10 am
The male has had another fight in the paddock The other Male blackbird flew off after about 2 minutes.

12.15 pm
Male singing on the roof. The female is incubating the second clutch. This is unusual because the young blackbirds are fed by both parents, then when they leave them, then the female starts to lay another clutch.

May 29th Wednesday   9 am
Male seen with beakful of worms feeds them to the female who is incubating the second cluth of eggs. The male is singing strongly in the mornings around 8 to 9 a.m. and at dinnertime around 11.30 to 1.30 he is also singing late in the evening around 9 p.m.

May 30th Thursday
First brood are still around the male's territory I have only seen 3 when there should be 5. 8.30 pm. Still feeding them. Female is off the nest and has a fight with a male blackbird she did not look as though she had suffered any wounds. It was in the paddock.

May 31st Friday
One of the first brood has been killed by a cat only 4 left. Female is still incubating the second clutch.

The diary continues throughout June. Then comes a heading: *Answers to my questions*

1   my answer to question one is on the territorial map.
2   *Their food diet*

Their food consists of mainly fruit grown in gardens and also wild fruit and they had the buds off apple and pear trees. they fed the young on mainly insects, earthworms etc.

3 *The males singing post*
When he is singing his favourite singing post is on our roof always facing north or east but never west or south. My answer is that the two most aggressive males are to the north and east whereas the less aggressive are to the south and west.

4 *Song difference from other males*
It is hard to tell really because each song is a little different from the other songs. His song is deep and he sings in shorter bursts of song than the other surrounding male birds.

5 *Which bird incubates the eggs?*
The female does all the incubating she gets off the nest every early morning and at dusk to feed and exercise her wings.

6 *Behaviour of male towards the female*
The males atitued towards the female is gentle and friendly and I didn't see any aggression against each other.

7 *Behaviour of male towards other females*
The aggression is mostly turned to the males but the male blackbird did show aggressive behaviour towards females sometimes.

8 *How does the male defend his territory?*
He defends it mainly by song but he has had fights over it mainly when the female was incubating the eggs.

9 *Are there special feeding times?*
No, there isn't they feed when is nessersary and only take the adequate amount.

10 *Does the male have any special singing times?*
Yes, he is singing mainly early in the morning singing around midday and then again in the evening. Each time he sings no more than 45 minutes.

Tim's biology teacher had written: 'This is very good indeed Tim. A most exciting study. Well done!' We would agree. There is no doubt that the writer in this instance is very much involved in his own learning, collecting his own data from his own observations – because he wants to find out more than he knows already. Having noted down what he saw in his diary, he can then reflect on these observations in order to answer the questions that initiated the study.

In the next set of observations we can see a second year girl attempting to make sense of what she sees (along with her friend) by interpreting it in the light of what she already knows. The writing offers plenty of scope to the teacher to take the girls' speculations further in discussion. Speculation invites discussion, especially where the pupils have been truly caught up in considering possibilities. Again, we only have space for a couple of excerpts from the detailed notes that this girl made. The writing is dominantly transactional, focussed on what is happening but we think that Nicolette's interest and involvement in what she is observing comes through. She goes further than just recording what she sees, she thinks about it and tries to work out its significance.

Communication with animals   Nicolette (12–13)

1 We put a rabbit on a table. He sniffed around and looked over the edge of the table. He twitched his nose and ears and he kept jumping onto a nearby box. Then we put two rabbits together. The Rabbit that we had first put on the table sniffed at the new rabbit, and they stayed close together twitching their ears and noses. Then we separated them they tried to get around the book which was dividing the table in two they tried to get over the book, and sniffed at the bottom and edges of it. We then let them go back together again, they didn't seem to take any notice of each other. So we think that Rabbits communicate by twitching their ears and nose. If they are frightened they jump and wriggle. We think that rabbits when they are alone and twitch their nose and ears, are communicating lonlyness, and when they are frightened they wriggle their tails and jump. They communicate friendliness when they lick and nibble one another.

2 We put 1 male and 1 female rabbit together. At first they didn't seem to take any notice of each other. Then the male sniffed around the female. They then stood close to each other. The male rabbit went into a hunched up position and

his cheeks quivered. They then nibbled each other not in enemy terms though. We think it is their way of showing affection to each other. They stayed close together and continued nibbling each other. The male rabbit looked over the edge of the table he ran back to the female jumped into the air and shook his head. They then stayed close together. Then they explored together. The male washed and his cheeks began to quiver as if he were speaking without any sound. He nosed the female and nibbled her. He then stuck his toung out and waggled it about. He then had another wash. The female stayed nearby but she didn't seem to take much notice of him. Then she put her head onto his back, and they kept close together. Then the male licked the female.

These sort of observations continue for another couple of pages in Nicolette's exercise book. She has a final note:

About the rabbits
The rabbits we used for these experiments were 6 weeks old. They all lived together, but they are two different families. Three boy dutch rabbits and two girl angora rabbits.

The assumptions that Nicolette and her friend make about how these rabbits communicate with each other are often anthropomorphic. They are projecting what they know about human communication onto their observations of the rabbits, for instance, 'The male washed and his cheeks began to quiver as if he were speaking without any sound' or 'The male rabbit looked over the edge of the table he ran back to the female jumped into the air and shook his head.' It is understandable that the girls are transposing what they know of human behaviour onto rabbit behaviour; the writing however makes it possible for a teacher to probe them more searchingly about their assumptions: how, for instance, can we be sure that facial movements like quivering cheeks and tongues sticking out have any connection with the way rabbits behave towards each other? Such gestures may be significant but extensive further observation would be necessary before a definite connection could be established.

The girls' observations here could lead them to think further about the nature of communication — how far do we all rely on visual expressions to convey what we feel, and how far has the ability of human beings to use language given them certain important advantages over non-verbal animals? The girls could be encouraged to continue their project by observing some human animals inter-relating with each other (round a table if not on it!): they could compare their first set of observations with what they noticed on this occasion.

If Nicolette and her friend are able to understand the need for further study then they will already have learnt a lot. Formulating a hypothesis 'we think . . . ' is often a long way from arriving at the conclusion 'we think' and as yet the girls are not able to make a clear distinction between the two. How we know and what the differences are between 'knowing' and 'guessing' are important educational questions. Nicolette's attempts to make sense of what she sees, though, have started her off on a very productive line of thought.

The difficulties of drawing on secondary sources

All the 'engaged' pieces that we have used so far have been based on information derived from first-hand experience. There is no doubt that it is easier for a pupil to feel that he has information that is worth communicating when it is based on what he has noticed for himself. For one thing he is aware that the teacher is not already in possession of the facts before he even starts to write about them. A fourth year girl told us that she felt there was some point to writing down what she had thought and felt about old people because 'I don't think there's anything in the project that she (the teacher) really knew about. I mean she knows about old age and that, but it's mainly my opinions about old age and what I've found out. . . . '

Each of the pupils whose work we have just quoted was in that sort of position, and we think that their writing reflects the confidence that comes from having something to communicate which is drawn from their own observations. It is far more difficult for pupils to feel either confident or committed to information when it is really someone else's knowledge that they are drawing on and not their own.

Here for instance, are three pieces from Paul's first year humanities folder:

The lungfish   Paul (11–12)
In the lungfish the air bladder is modified to serve as a lung so that they breathe air when out of water as well as tacking in dissolved oxygen. This helps them to live through periods of drought or in stagnant marshes. The lungfish is found in South america, Australia and South Africa. It feeds on slow moving bottom fish.

Why reptiles are an improvement on amphibians
For one reason reptiles are better for laying eggs. Reptiles can lay on land Amphibians lay in the water. So when the eggs hatch the reptiles are not useto to land Amphibians are not.
Reptiles usually live in caves they eat insects and a little larger animals. They have quite large teeth. Their eyes are on the side of their head, their legs are quite short their skin is quite rough. There is not many Amphibians left There are frogs Salamanders and newts.

Teacher's comment: Fair attempt but . . . A difficult way to answer the question, especially as you have missed out several important points.

The elephant (Reproduction)
The length of the gestation period is twenty to twenty two months, and there is only one calf a birth. Rarely twins. Birth is generally quick and with very little pain, In spite of the size of the foetus. Dropped onto soft damp ground or a bed of leaves, it lies for a few hours before standing up. lactation continues for months after the young has begun to eat grass. Elephant milk is very sweet and rich in cream. Growth appears to be rapid. One elephant weighted 650 pounds at the age of fifteen months and was 3′ 8″ tall. Two years later it weighed 1,610 pounds and measured 5′ 3″ Inches.

We might ask ourselves whether Paul learnt anything new as a result of putting this information down in writing that he had not already gained from his reading. In his first and third pieces he is drawing on the words of another writer, like Jane when she wrote her Lighthouse Project. The second piece shows the teacher how clearly Paul can now distinguish between reptiles and amphibians; his writing shows that he is still not very clear on how reptiles are an improvement – but is still at the stage of noting differences. Unfortunately the teacher's comment doesn't help to take him further. It notes his failure without suggesting another way of looking at the facts.

Again, we can't really tell from this writing whether Paul was interested in any of these creatures. Like Jane and Claire he doesn't appear to be doing anything with the information he has gathered other than reproducing it somewhat haphazardly for the teacher. There is no framework or perspective on his part which endows the facts with some significance. By contrast, Debbie, Tim and Nicolette were already interested in birds and animals before they ever began writing. They were actively using what they already knew (their own observations, views and expectations) to make sense of new material. They run the risk of being wrong – of making illogical or premature judgments – but because they want to know, such errors can become the source of fresh learning.

There is another major difference between writing which is drawn from first-hand experience and writing which is drawn from books. In the former instance the writer has to find his own words for what he wants to say; in writing that is drawn from secondary sources words have usually been found already by someone else. At a first glance this might appear to make the writing easier – but we do not believe this to be the case, because in effect, they represent another writer's perceptions and not those of the 'new' learner.

In our next piece, although Jennifer had seen a film and read a teacher's booklet about Galileo, we detect an inability to find a pattern in the facts which has much meaning for her. It is rather as though she is trying to fit together the scattered pieces of an unfamiliar jigsaw puzzle. But they are still all jumbled and confused.

Galileo   Jennifer (11–12)
Galileo was a great mathmatishion. When he was young he

studed the stars and worked out that the heaviest thing would reach the gound at the same time as the lightest thing which he dropped. He worked very hard, tring with experiments important kinds of things. One day when some people were having a feast with him a man began to qarral with him about the experiments. And to make a long story short I will carry on from when he was an old man.

He was an old man, still tring to carry on with his experiments and was not imprisoned in his own home. He was cripiling in his arms and legs, so he could not walk propeley. He was taken to a kind of church and had to neal on a cushion and swear off of a book that he would not teatch in any way about the things he had learned, but he had swearn and would not give up all the work he had done.

Galileo was a great beliver in science. Galileo was born in pisa, Italy. He went to a school, which was a monastry of Vallombrosa. He was 25 when he dropped all of his subjects and took up science. He became famous, I think. Galileo went to the top of the leaning tower of pisa.

This writing indicates more clearly than any of the pieces we have used so far, that Jennifer just hasn't been able to take on someone else's knowledge 'complete'. She is still very much at the beginning of the reconstructing process that is necessary if these items of information are to be converted for her, into coherent knowledge. Whether she continues that process any further will depend on many factors – including whether she has experienced any spark of real interest in Galileo or his discoveries and perhaps as importantly, the extent to which her teacher values these first efforts to form a picture or dismisses them as inadequate.

How can teachers help?
What can we do as teachers of subjects which do not readily stem from our pupils' personal experience, to create an interest which will motivate them to think about new information instead of simply stockpiling it on a short-term basis? How can we encourage them to begin reconstruing for themselves rather than reproducing for use? We want now to consider some of the approaches to this problem

that seem to have succeeded in encouraging children to use written language to make their own way into new information which has either partly or entirely been drawn from secondary sources.

One way that we have mentioned already, is to make a conscious effort to provide our pupils with an audience which enables them to write what they really think without being constantly criticised about it; for a reader in other words who will pay real regard to the way it looks through their eyes. We believe that it is just as important for the teacher to provide this kind of sympathetic audience in subjects such as history, geography and science as it is in the more traditionally 'personal' subjects such as English and religious education. Let us look at two more pieces from the second year logs written for the humanities teacher that we quoted from briefly in chapter one. We see here from his written comments how he is trying to help some second year pupils to make links between the information that he has been presenting to them and interests or experiences which they already possess. His concern as the teacher-reader is not so much that they should faithfully reflect what they have been told as that some of it should actually set them thinking.

Andrew (Excerpt from his log for 'Enquiry' lessons)
One thing I didn't like about the industrial Revolution when it came, was the employing of children in factories. They were given dangerous jobs like going under machines which were in motion. And children which had to work in the coal mines I feel bad about this because when they worked they never went to school and so they grew up they weren't able to read or write. I learn things and am able to write about a certain subject by reading a book or if the teacher reads it out aloud. I myself do a lot of reading at home but since we got a television I don't do as much as I would like to. I have got an interest in writing plays, I have written two already and acted them with the help of a few friends and a tape. I think it's because of the challenge of writing a good one that makes me interested in them.

Teacher: How could you bring your thoughts about the Industrial Revolution and your interest in playwriting together?

Andrew
A good question, I suppose I could write a play of something out of the industrial Revolution like children working in factories, or about a group of them who try and runaway because they are so fed up with the misery of working in the factory. Or even children who are working in the coal mines. I think that would be a good way of bringing the two subjects together, although it would take a lot of work on my part I should think, because I would have to create the right atmosphere of it all and sense what the children feel. Anyway, now I think I'll finish off and give my mind a rest, although I would go on if I could and finish this page but I've got nothing else to say.

Dennis
This term in enquiry, we have studied:
the countryside, farming, the way people used to live in the countryside, the Enclosures and how working people came to live in the towns and work in the factories we also looked at inventions, transport and roads, the condition of work in factories and coal mines, iron, building and power and finally life in the towns.
We learnt about museum, farming, combien, countryside, What I have learnt in school. I learnt about museum, combien, countryside, milling tank, cornfield, wheat to make flour, cows and sometime I does feel intreted in what the teacher say but not everything I can that at the same time.
By lessoning all what the teacher said

Teacher: What have you been interested in?

I am interested in power, iron and William Wilkins.

Teacher: Who was William Wilkins?

He was a poor farmer and have a wife and two children. The next farmer get the richer land and he will get the bad part of the land.

Teacher: Yes, what feelings do you have about what happened to him?

He and his family will went to the towns with they cows in the big pasture for his cows to get food to eat because he did not have very big lands so he had was to went to the towns and get a job in factory if was me I would feel angry because I don't have lands every morning I have to wake up. and if I had two cows I wouldn't like to go in peoples land and fed it.
I . . .
I wouldn't like to go in the factory and look for a work for me an my family (me?) is a strager. I just like to get my job to do.

Teacher: When we studied farming you told us all about the countryside and farming in Granada. Then you came to England. What is it like to be a stranger – do you think *you* felt any of the things that William Wilkins might have felt?

I felt lonely at school because I dont have no friends to talk with. I will say to in my mind what I come to England for. but after I will . . . start getting interested in the work I do in school. When I was in Granada, I live in the country with my friends we will go to the mountain and cut grass for we cows in the fields in one day time we will cut about 12 pal of grass and I if we dont cut 12 pal of grass we mum will bit. we every morning before we go to school we have to go in the mountain and cut six pal of grass some time we rich late to school

Here we can see how the teacher deliberately focusses Dennis' attention on the way he *feels* about the facts – what they mean to him in terms of his own experience. His comments to both boys are not just about their work, they are about the next steps that each could take to penetrate the facts further. The teacher's capacity to make such connections between what he knows of the child and what he knows of the subject are at the heart of his job as an educator. If he can encourage his pupils to find points of contact between the unfamiliar and the known – in their own terms and in the context of their own needs and interests – he will be helping them to extend their insights into the world around them and their own relation to it, which after all is what teaching is all about.

If teacher and taught are able to enter into a genuinely co-operative relationship the learning is by no means all one sided. If he is attentive to how his pupils reach out towards new knowledge, the teacher will himself continue to learn about learning – there are also many occasions on which he may also learn to look differently at the work on which they are engaged together.

Here, for instance, is a brief excerpt from a teacher's account of the weekly visits that one of his students was making to a local primary school and how they both learnt from her experience:

Six weeks have passed since our first visit to Dunton Basset and I can begin to reflect on what each of us has achieved so far out of our experience. Part of Carol's achievement, I think, is to have rediscovered her own childhood. It may even be just because she has discovered her own childhood that she has also discovered how to enter imaginatively into the childhood of others and so how to talk out of experience and intuition and in part out of reflecting on experience and intuition in talk and in writing.

As for me, I feel that, reading what Carol has written, talking over her experience with her, and spending some time in the same classroom myself, has enriched my understanding of how to observe children and how to create relationships with them, in ways which I would have not discovered for myself.

Our next piece is taken from some earlier work of Carol's that she did in the fifth year at school. This time the starter for her own thinking was a worksheet about the Cuttleslowe walls. What it sparks off in Carol is a reaction to what she has thought *up to now* about social discrimination. Reading about the situation in Oxford, she is impelled to try and relate it to her own views about social class and social discrimination:

The Cuttleslowe walls   Carol (15–16)
On reading about the Cutteslowe walls I think it was a very

terrible thing for the government to even think about putting a wall between the two estates, the person who built the two estates should have realised what would have happened, I also think to put a person in a so called class is pompus.

When talking to a person about social class they alway's class people by there way of living, eg. housing, if you class a person who lives in a big luxurious house, as upper class or middle class person, and a person who lives on a council estate a lower class of person it is totally wrong. To be even put in a class you need a job, so a person works very hard to become an executive and doesn't like it, but wants to be there because it puts him in an upper class position yet another person finds a job as a rail-wayman and loves his job yet he is still classed as lower class or working class, anyway thats straying away from the Cutteslowe Walls a bit so to go back to the two estates.

If one estate is working class and another middle class why do the middle class have the better because the working class didn't exactly mix together with the working class so why all the difference, I'm sure the working class wouldn't mone about living next to middle class people so why should the middle class mone about living next to council tenants? Then we come back to classing if people hadn't started classing themselves better off as others the walls would never have happened.

The Area in which the walls were was similar to the area where I live for a start there are council houses which we don't think them as *council houses*, but as somewhere we live, then at the bottom of our road is some more houses which are far far better than the council houses I think they are town houses and they cost a bomb. Then a couple of yards away from the council houses and the town houses, are the proper middle class people well thats what they think they are, but to me they are all human beings, and I don't know them from the lower class to upper class. And if there was a wall put up between us I couldn't care less as long as it wasn't our idea.

In some ways this writing is similar to Jennifer's Galileo piece in so far as both girls are in the early stages of sorting out their thoughts; the crucial difference seems to be that Carol feels strongly about the injustice of social discrimination and wants to let her teacher know what she thinks where Jennifer has not really felt the injustices suffered by Galileo at all. She has read about them and seen them portrayed in a film but they don't appear as yet to have sparked off her own thinking in relation to that situation in the way that Carol's thoughts have been activated by reading about the Walls.

Thinking imaginatively

The linked processes which we refer to as imagining and speculating, can also help children to make sense of new information which they cannot easily (or even possibly) experience directly. In one of our earlier Project papers called *Do Historical Stories Have to Get It Right?* we put forward the view that in historical studies the past always has to be *envisaged* if it is to be meaningful. We would extend this need for a three-dimensional reconstruction of a world from basic facts to any exploration of either the past, future or present where it is outside our own experience. If pupils are encouraged to put themselves in the picture they are more likely to perceive the significance of the facts at their disposal. It is one thing to 'know' for instance, that Wedgwood organised his workers to specialise in a particular process in the making of a pot, but without imagining the effects of such specialisation on the men involved, the information is only half realised.

We believe that the mental act of envisaging or imagining (which we do continuously in conversation about people, events and ideas) has in school work been largely restricted either to the exploration of personal fantasies in English lessons or to the lower forms or lower streams as a mental activity which is regarded as inferior (when information is being dealt with) to generalising about the facts and to ordering them logically and concisely. We wouldn't claim to understand fully what happens when children's imagination is brought into play, but in its widest sense we would regard imagination as that mental process which enables a person to make his own connections, whether this happens to be in the sciences or in the arts. It may be that those moments are rare when an 'imaginative leap' opens up new patterns and new perspectives for others, but unless we provide many opportunities all over the curriculum for children to use their imaginations more extensively, their knowledge will remain inert.

We would like to end this chapter with four pieces of work in which students have had to draw upon their imaginations in order to perceive more fully the significance of the information which they had already acquired either from the teacher or from a textbook. Jackie, who produced the first piece, is in the same class as the girl who wrote the Wedgwood notes. On this occasion however, their history teacher had asked them to incorporate the facts that they had been given about conditions in 19th century workhouses into a piece called 'My first day in the workhouse'. This request was relatively unusual because it was made to a fifth year o level group. Most students wrote at greater length than they did normally and the teacher was very pleased with the result. Jackie's piece is fairly typical:

My first day in the workhouse   Jackie (15–16)
I woke up on a hard bed with a sheet hardly the size of myself strewn across my body. The bell rang through my head, it rang and rang 'Get up you lazy rat no sympathy for new 'uns' was bellowed at me. A push from behind and I was on the hard stone floor. It was cold and burned my skin. I got up and walked towards the crowd gathering at the door. We all had brown smock-like dresses on but the older people had thinner holey ones where they had obviously worked harder.
We were all told to go to a room the name of which I didn't catch. Everyone hurried along to the dark damp room where more people, mostly females crouched over wooden tables and ate a sloppy broth that was obviously nasty. We all spread around the wooden tables and in turn collected a bowl from one table and a ladle full of the lumpy food. I sat on the long wooden bench between a young girl who, like the others looked very sad but she had tears in her eyes. On the other side of me sat an older lady about 50 years of age who smelt stale and occasionally broke from slurping her broth to comb her greying hair with her thin dirty hands. The broth was sour and only just warm I forced it down my throat knowing it was probably the first meal for some hours.
I turned my attention towards the girl. She was thin and tears were streaming down her high cheekbones. 'What's up' I said

hoping to make friends with someone as soon as possible.

She stared at me as though it was my fault and then looked away again.

'Er brothers in the punishment room, 'e was caught drinkin, poor soul, treat ya bad 'ere ya know, ever bin in a workhouse before then' it was the woman from the other side of me who had nudged me from behind.

'No,' I answered 'never'

'Well you'll have to learn not to speak to your family or they'll punish ya too see' she said scraping her bowl with her hands.

We were all filed out in two different groups, some were to 'do the ropes' the others were to 'do breaking'. I was to do the ropes. Some people were to clear up after the meal and were picked at random. It shocked me that everyone's faces were showing no emotion at all.

I wondered as I walked into a small stone room what the rest of the family were doing. My brother was in a different part of the building and my mother wasn't around at breakfast – we'd been split up.

Doing the ropes was splitting up old ropes to the smallest possible amount. It was a tedious job, my nails broke and my fingers were red. If anyone communicated they were either beaten or dragged out if it was often. After what seemed twelve hours work we had a break. We were all sent into a yard where the older people slouched against the wall. I talked to the lady who had spoken to me at breakfast and learned that we got up at 6, worked until one (this was one), and worked right through until 6 again. Then we went back to the room where we ate another meal which was usually a broth again and a chunk of cheese.

I saw my mother while wandering around the grey dark yard but when I approached her we were split up and she was beaten. It was so cruel. I looked around as I sat picking at the ropes, wondering how much I was going to see of this room and how much I would end up hating it. Was my life really going to carry on in this gloomy, cold grey building with monotonous work and hard beds. No friends, nothing to enjoy and no personal life, now I could see the reason for all the unemotional faces.

Jackie has recreated in imagination a world in which she can project herself into the feelings of the human beings that people it. The question that she is asking herself – which provides a focus for the facts about the food and the regulations and the work – is 'What would it *feel* like to find oneself in such a situation?' In order to answer her question, the facts that she has read or been told have to be taken into account – but now their significance lies in the effect they have on the wretched folk who have to put up with them: 'now I could see the reason for all the unemotional faces'. And in making this connection she has drawn on her own experience of misery and thereby drawn knowledge from books into the area of first-hand experience.

In the next piece, a second year boy is envisaging the chain of possible happenings which might have led to discoveries being made by primitive people. The class had been doing experiments in the lab with different mineral ores and their teacher had suggested that for homework they might imagine how the properties of copper were first discovered.

Grog   Philip (12–13)

My name is Grog I live in a little village near a river. One day I made a fire place using some big stones which had some turquoise streaks in them. That night I lit a fire with my flints and kept it going all night. It was a lovely big fire and I roasted meat on it. Next morning I was woken up by my son who had been playing with the embers of the fire. He came in shouting 'father, father, look what I've found in the fire.' He showed me a sort of orange-brown coloured substance. I immediately thought it was a gift from the gods so I took it to the chief who was amazed, and burnt it as a sacrifice, but instead of burning it melted and ran down the altar and dropped into a jug. We thought this meant the gods didn't want our sacrifice.

Later we decided to get the 'copper' as we decided to call it, out of the jug. But it was set solid, so we broke the jug open and it was the shape of the jug. The chief who was a wise man decided to make a hole in the ground the shape of a knife and again sacrifice the metal and the liquid copper melted and ran into the shape in the earth. Later it was set and we took it out and

rubbed it on a stone to make it shine and low and behold it became sharp. 'If only we had more of this copper we could stop the northern tribes from killing us so easily because of there strength in numbers', said the chief.
Later that day I was sitting outside my hut when I noticed the rocks that had turquoise streaks now had pink streaks. I began to think. I thought the copper might have come from the rocks not the gods. So I put some more rocks round my fire and did the same thing. Next day I found more copper. So I told the chief and the whole village did what I had done. And we all made knives spear heads axe heads arrow heads and swords. And we beat the northern tribes in a great battle.

What Philip has achieved in this short piece is a combination of information, speculation and story-telling. The story provides the framework within which he is hypothesising that this might have caused that to happen, and so on: 'Later we decided to get the "copper" as we decided to call it, out of the jug. But it was set solid, so we broke the jug open and it was the shape of the jug'. It is a genuine story (look at the way it ends) and we shall have more to say about writing like this which has moved into the poetic function in the next chapter. We would just like to note here how the use of his imagination has enabled the writer to explore the topic in a multi-faceted way.

The remaining two pieces were both produced in response to the teacher inviting the class to use their imaginations speculatively. In both cases, the invitation was designed to make them consider possibilities in as open a way as they were able. It was hoped that the issues thus raised would highlight the significance of the information that the teacher was subsequently going to present to them.

In the first instance, the class (third year) was about to study the Russian revolution, but initially they were asked to imagine how they would organise a successful revolution in their own school. Some of the pupils tackled this by plunging into fantasy ('The head-master has a private study lined with furs and on the wall there are trophies of when he was in India'); others wrote a narrative account as though the revolution had actually happened ('In the meeting we held, we allocated different jobs to certain people to suit what they were good at'); others after preliminary discussion were more hypothetical about it:

School revolution   Martin (13–14)

If 3M organised a revolution in the school this is how I would go about it.

First I would try to win the support of the rest of the school. I would use such reasons as, there is nothing to do in the lunch-times, too much difficult homework etc.

The next thing I would do would be to cut the telephone wires and seal off the school. At all the exits there would be about 10 people guarding them armed with weapons that had (been) smuggled in or made. Such as air rifles, 12 bore shotguns, dartguns, 4 × 10 shotguns, .22 hunting rifles etc. Or weapons such as knives, javelins, clubs, bats, darts etc from the sports department.

After rounding up all the teachers we would lock them up and guard them. We would then give our ultimatum to the head-master. Saying if he didn't sign a legal paper saying these things would be corrected, every hour a teacher would be shot in the head in front of him.

To overcome problems such as the pupils turning against us, we would say that when this was over the tuckshop and canteen would be unlocked and everybody could have as much as they could take. On the roofs would be snipers armed with .22 hunting rifles to shoot any teacher who tries to escape. The perimeter of the school grounds would be patrolled by dogs and 12 bore armed pupils. The parents and pedestrians would not suspect a thing because forged letters which had been circulated the previous day had said that we were holding a *mock* revo-lution. And by hometime everything would be back to normal.

As far as we know 3M haven't had their revolution yet, but it seems likely to us that the encouragement to plan for it would increase the interest of the group in the events that actually took place in Russia at the time of the revolution there – and also their insight into 'why?' and 'how?'

Our final illustration of how children can be encouraged to make sense of facts is an example of imaginative thinking but it is not in this instance, expressed verbally. The class (second year) were asked to design an X machine after discussion in groups about how this should be done; they were then given this worksheet:

Introduction to programme of work on plants
This is an introduction to the work you will be doing during the next two weeks. It may seem a bit odd – or even slightly crazy, but we hope that by the end of the course, you will see the point of it and find it useful. What we are going to ask you to do is difficult, but try to do your very best.

What to do
Imagine that the world of science fiction is in fact *real*. Imagine that scientists have managed to design and build machines that can repair themselves, and more important, *provide their own fuel*, all without man's help. What would such a machine look like?

We want you to try and answer this question by designing two machines yourself. You will work in groups. Paper on which you should draw your design will be provided. Now, here are the two machines:

The X machine
The special thing about this machine is that it gets all it needs from a supply of water, air and light.
What would this machine look like if it was designed to get as much of these things as possible?

The Y machine
The special thing about this machine is that it gets what it needs by taking materials from *other* machines (a bit like a factory which uses steel from old motor cars to make new refrigerators). Remember that the machine must be able to get hold of the materials it needs without man's help.
What would this machine look like, if it is to be good at doing its job?

What to write

1 When your group have agreed on the designs, make neat full-page drawings of them.
2 Label the drawings to explain what the different parts are for.
3 Show your design to your teacher. We plan to prepare *final* versions of the designs from each tutor group; these will be displayed in the large area.

AND WHAT IS THE POINT OF IT ALL? THAT IS WHAT WE ARE ABOUT TO FIND OUT.

We can only include designs for the 'light, water and air' machine because the group had not reached the stage of Y machines when

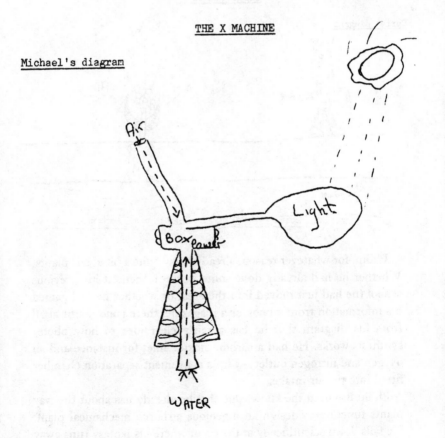

THE X MACHINE

Michael's diagram

we were in the school. But we think the teacher's decision to introduce the work on plants and animals in this way raises some interesting points. By inviting the children's own ideas about how such a machine would work, the teacher was hoping to draw on knowledge which they already possessed. Their efforts to formulate a design would perhaps focus what they knew into a pattern which would then throw light on the basic elements of plant construction. Most of the class did in fact design machines with drills rather like roots to suck up water, and larger open surfaces to take in light and air. Michael's diagram is typical of many in this respect. Chris's drawing shows how already he was relating what he knew to plant structure as well as to his machine.

THE X MACHINE

Chris' diagram

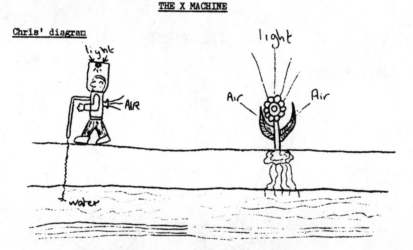

Philip, for whatever reason, already knew quite a bit about plants. Whether he had already done some work on them at his previous school (he had just moved into the area) or whether he had gained his information from a book or a magazine, there is no doubt at all from his diagram that he has a fairly clear idea of how photosynthesis works. He had a carbon dioxide inlet for instance and an oxygen and nitrogen outlet – with a convenient separation chamber fitted into the air intake.

Philip has used the knowledge that he already has about the way plants function to design an ingenious airborne mechanical plant. He falls down scientifically at the point where his fantasy runs away with him, but the distinction between an imaginative reconstruction controlled by a scientific purpose and speculation running away into fantasy is not easy to maintain. So, as well as demonstrating how the machine converts light, water and air into power for itself, he goes one further and suggests that the x machine also produces food: 'This machine produces food in tablet form. It is pollution free.'

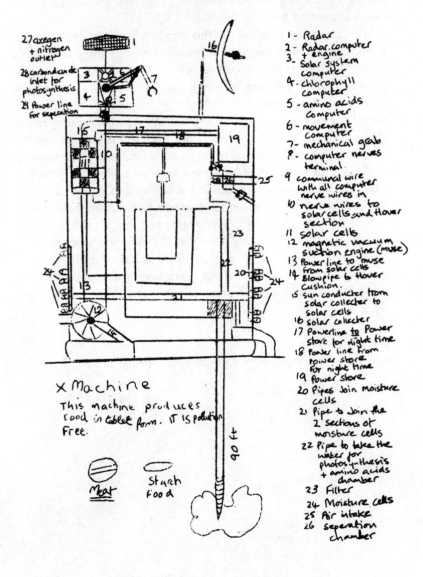

This is more a flight of fancy that a serious imaginative concept, as there is nothing in the diagram to substantiate either of these statements.

But we don't want to end this chapter with a quibble. Philip's machine is highly ingenious and in large part succeeds imaginatively in demonstrating the significance of the information that he is dealing with. Our guess would be that he enjoyed inventing it – and that is important too.

We have tried to show in this chapter how children can be encouraged to make sense of new information *by using it to think with*. The teacher's own concept of what constitutes learning is bound to affect the range of opportunities that are offered to his pupils to find their own 'ways in' to what is new and unfamiliar, so that it begins to make sense to them. If he regards learning as the kind of process defined by the Bullock team in the passage that we quoted earlier in the chapter (p. 67), then he will search for ways of working with his students that make an ongoing dialogue possible, whatever his subject specialism in the curriculum. In our work for the Project we have been on the constant look out for writing that has helped to take the writer further into real insights about himself and his world. We can only hope that the examples given here, in which the pupil's own thoughts and feelings have been involved in making sense of new information, have helped to suggest some of the possibilities that a 'reconstructive' approach to learning can offer.

References
DES (1975) *A Language for Life* (Bullock Report) HMSO

Chapter four

Sharing feelings and shaping them

When we ask children what kinds of writing they enjoy doing, mostly they say 'stories'. We have also come across others who write poems from choice, at home as well as at school, including so-called 'remedial' students. In this chapter we want to consider in more detail what doors poems and stories are able to open for children, what gives them such a powerful appeal?

Traditionally, 'poetic' or 'creative' or 'personal' writing in secondary schools has been regarded largely as the preserve of the English teacher. In English lessons children have always read and listened to stories and poems so it has seemed appropriate that English lessons should be the place where they write them. It is probably still true that most poems and stories by children over the age of eleven or twelve are written in this context, but increasingly as English becomes involved in Integrated Studies or Humanities courses, the opportunities widen for encouraging children to think, talk and write personally and imaginatively – not as a diversion from learning but as a means of arriving at further understanding.

In this chapter we want to consider in more detail what happens when children choose or are encouraged to write in the poetic function. What is the writer concentrating on when he begins a story or a poem? Our short answer would be his feelings – his feelings in relation to the scene in front of him, or to the memories he is evoking of some past experience or to what he can imagine of other people's lives, or to events that move him, but at the heart of any writing which is poetic in function it will be *a felt response* that is expressed.

Re-shaping experience
Often children will begin moving in this direction in their writing

when they return to experiences which already in real life have held some significance for them. By recollecting these, they are re-activating thoughts and feelings which for many reasons may have affected them powerfully. Sometimes of course they choose to re-create such experiences in talk – or paint or music. But when writing is the medium, what emerges is usually a poem or a story or more often a piece of personal, expressive writing which is potentially a story or a poem. (We have restricted our comments to poems and stories for the following reasons: in our work we have come across very few examples of children's writing which have taken the form of a scripted play. Mostly, extended pieces of dialogue are incorporated within the narrative framework of a story. It may be that children prefer to make plays with spoken language. We would also suggest tentatively, that by its nature a play is a different kind of literary construct from either poems or stories in that it is rarely intended to stand on its own in print.)

The 'audience' and 'function' writing dimensions which we described in chapter one have helped us to trace how poetic writing develops from relatively unformed expressive pieces, in which the child is willing to share some of his experiences by putting them onto paper. We all *tell* anecdotes about ourselves to our friends quite spontaneously because sharing them validates our own experience and confirms our sense of identity and mattering to other people. Personal writing can serve a similar purpose if children can trust the teacher to respond in much the same way as friends do – with genuine interest and possibly amusement or sympathy.

Of course as the shaping of such anecdotes becomes more skilled, the need for such a known and trusted audience decreases. You will probably notice this audience difference between some of the writings here. The pieces which are dominantly expressive would almost certainly mean more to you if you knew the children who had written them and could picture their faces, personalities and the way they might come up and talk to you in school. The dominantly poetic pieces on the other hand, can be appreciated as stories and poems in their own right by a wider public audience because the writers have been able to move from anecdote to art.

Our first two pieces are both expressive. Each boy is recollecting an experience, re-working it and re-shaping it as he writes. Neither finds written language an easy medium to work with but in spite of that both pieces convey an awareness and an appreciation of the experience as they remember it which transforms what must have been an uncomfortable few moments into an enjoyable anecdote. We would like to note in passing, a point we shall come back to later, the remarkable ability of literature even in its most elementary form to change an unpleasant experience into a pleasant one.

A new responsibility Chris (12–13)

Some time ago when I was about 10 I was left at home to look after the house wilst my mouther went down to the shops, with my sisters. I was left alone in the house I was watching. a program on the television when there was a knok on the door. I only opened the door a small way and I saw a man from the builders down in herbert Road. he said are your parents in I said no. then he said well weve brou the cement. and sand your parents ordered but I said but we dont want any cement and sand then he said they must have ordered it they haven't. I said then he went away. I closed the door then he came back and waved a peace of yellow paper in the air. he was very cross when I said we don't want any cement. and sand. then he said hers the profe then I said it again that we didn't want any cement and sand. then I closed the door and went up stars and watched. What was happening. through on of the windows. the lory went off I thought they were going but they weren't. they were just manovoing the lory so they could dump the sand and cement. they put it at the end of the drive way. I didn't no wate to do so I took down their number and the firm which owned the lory the only thing I could right it on was on of my mums handkerchiefs. Later the man how realy wanted the cement and sand came and tuck it away he said he lived at number 11 mere worth drive and I live at number 14 mereworth drive and so the firm how brought the stuph Must have made a mistake in the number.

A near miss Raymond (13–14)

One day last week I desided to get some dandilions for my rabbit it was too far to walk so got on my bike and was just about to go out of the gate when I notist my front wheele was loose so I took it in home and tightened I up when Id finished my dad desided that it could do with a little oil the oil can sometimes works and sometimes doesent so my dad made sure that it worked so he took the clip off my wheel and started to pump the oil in but he did not think that it was working because it wasent coming out round the hole so he kept pumping until some did not to his knowing the oil had been coming out all the time and the wheele was abserlootly full with oil the same happened to the back wheele it was getting late so I waited until Id had my tea after Id had my tea I got on my bike and started down the road by this time the oil had ran down the spokes and onto the wheele rims I went to stop at the lights I suddenly found out I had no breakes I could not stop so I went streat over the lights on red I swerved to avoid a lorry and missed it by inches I fell off my bike and screased my ancle but I was glad to get away with that I got some dandilions for my rabbit and walked home it was just over 2 miles so I was worn out by the time I got home the next day I took my bicicle wheeles to pieses and found that they were flooded with oil it took me all weekend to clean it out so now I keep it well away from my dad I think he had better stick to his car my self that way I can be safe and he can only hurt his self

Both pieces are linked closely to each boy's memories of what happened. Developmentally, 'A near miss' is moving closer to a story than 'A new responsibility' because Raymond shapes his recollections more deliberately, describing for instance how the wheels became 'abserlootly full with oil' without his father noticing. He brings his tale to a conclusion with rather more of a flourish too. In these respects, Raymond's writing is further along our spectrum towards the poetic.

The next piece which Julie wrote about herself, again drawing directly and explicitly on her own experience, may be further along still. This is no anecdote; she is aware that she is writing a poem and she has perceived the integrating quality in a series of experiences and is expressing those perceptions in her writing:

My half world   Julie (14–15)

I can't understand what people think,
What they are saying,
What their feelings and thoughts are towards me.
To me they seem as if they're in a different world.
Their world seems so alive
And mine is so still,
As though I'm in a still world.
I can't express the way I feel to them in words,
They can't understand what I'm saying.
The way I let them know the way I feel
Is by painting my thoughts.
Different colours for my different thoughts,
Reds and blacks when I feel angry,
And soft creamy colours when I feel happy and gay.

Although this piece has many of the features of poetic writing, such as compression of thought through imagery, it is still closer to talk at times than to poetry. It shows very clearly how our model of writing functions cannot be applied like a litmus test – (blue for expressive, pink for poetic) – because there is no hard and fast line between one writing function and another. Our aim in using it is rather to understand more clearly if we can, the growth which comes from the search for meaning as people interact with each other and with their environment. The clearer such meanings become when they are set down in a written form the more the writing is likely to move out of the expressive function into the transactional or the poetic. But our insights come gradually, so that learning is often reflected in an overlap of functions such as we find in Julie's poem.

Exploring feelings through fantasy

Our concern, as we have said before, is with how writing can reflect or provide growth points for each individual. In 'My half world' Julie already has a fairly clear idea of what she wants to say about herself, but often children draw upon their experiences less directly, especially when their emotional preoccupations are operating subconsciously. Poems and stories often symbolise very powerful feelings which the child cannot deal with explicitly; this may be one of the reasons why children will listen avidly from a very early age to nursery rhymes and to stories about giants and witches and castles and forests which can give a shape in the fantasy that is woven, to some of their deepest fears and conflicts. There are many instances of children writing stories and poems at primary as well as secondary level, which mirror in this symbolic way the private world of their inner feelings.

Here is a story by a girl in her first year at a comprehensive school. One of her teachers had suggested after some course work on carboniferous forests that as one of a number of possible activities the class could write a story about a forest or a swamp. It seems that in Corinne's case the invitation to write a story signalled that she could write what she wanted. She started writing immediately and when she arrived at her Humanities lesson the next day she was very keen to continue.

Her teacher told us: 'Corinne arrived in class the next day wanting to finish her story – did so while I was playing a tape. Obviously was excited by it and seemed to gain a lot of kudos from the length – the word flashed round the class "How much Corinne?" "Five!" ' It is quite apparent when we look at the original version that this child is well behind most of her age group in her capacity to handle written language. For her it is still very much a matter of seeing through a glass darkly, but her absorption was such that on this occasion she persisted to the end – and an end there certainly is.

Corinne's story
On Sunday I decided to call on Gillian and I knocked on the door and her Mum said she wasn't up. I thought she (?) not be up. I said when will she be up? Her Mum said I don't know so I waited outside her house. I said that I could not wait to go to the forest. All (of) a sudden Gillian looked out the window.

Sample of original spelling
On Sunday I diside to calle (on) gillian and I Nocked on the door And Her mum said she want up I thort She (?) Not be up. I Said when will she Be up Her mum said I Dont No sow I Waned out side her house I said that I could No want to go the The Forist. all a sudun Gillian looked out the window.

(Then) she got up and got dressed (her)self and eat her breakfast. (She) put her coat on and came (out). We are going to the
woods. All right. So we went (?) We saw a animal. Now we will
go home a (?) and will camp out the night because it is the
holidays. Bring some grub. Soon we found a place (?) then we
had some chips and beans and eggs. Then we had a walk round
the forest and then we had our supper. We had hot chocolate
and biscuits. So we had our supper and then we read for a bit.
Then we said Lets go to bed so we did and we heard a (Muser?)
noise and we looked outside and there was no-one there. We
went back to bed. In the morning we had toast and tea for breakfast. Then we decided to stay till next Saturday so we did. We
went shopping to fetch some groceries. We had (hewer?)
dinner (had?) Potatoes Peas Carrots Meat gravy and a drink of
pop and we got our tea (?) and we had to peel potatoes to use.
We decided to have (stew?) for tea and then (?) did Then when
we had our tea on the stove we (went for) a walk round the
forest. We got lost (but) we could smell our stew so we followed
the smell. And then we had (come) back to the camp. We had
our tea (use?) It was 4 o'clock (?) a cup of coffee. Then we
washed and we remembered about the radio and we had to put
the radio on and then we said Lets go to the tent for a bit and
then we had something like our sweet and we put it in the tent.
Then we went to the shop and Gillian had a better idea. Gillian
said Shall we climb trees said Gillian and I said all right Gillian
lead the way Gillian said all right I lead the way so then I did.
Gillian said (I) am higher than you said Gillian. I said all right
then and I got down. Gillian said Mardy Bum so I said You
carry on playing and I will make supper. So I did. And I
shouted Gillian and she came. It was 10.30 pm and we went to
bed. And the next day was Saturday and we went home. Then
we went to bed and it was Saturday morning. We went to pack
up then we did and then we said Come on then. On the way out
of the forest (when) Gillian fell in a swamp. I tried to get some
rope but I could not find any and Gillian was gone.
       That (is) the end.

We recognise that Corinne has all kinds of problems. It is not just that she is very unsure in her handling of writing, about how words are spelt; the way she puts sentences together is jerky and uncertain and her grasp of narrative is very uncertain too. But in spite of these difficulties we think that Corinne is learning here how to make written words work for her. Her impulse to write and to explore her feelings about Gillian obliquely like this, seems to spring from her response to the notion of a 'story'. Perhaps the imagery of forests and swamps moved her subconsciously into fantasy. At any rate in her make believe world she can begin to work out the problems of her relationship with her best friend. Which of them is the boss? Which of them is 'best'? At one point, when Gillian claims to have climbed higher, Corinne stops competing and takes on the role of 'Mum' instead: 'I said you carry on playing and I will make supper'. This solution to their rivalry seems preferable to Gillian's total demise – although from the point of view of the story-maker that ending has a satisfactory air of finality about it.

We know from the context that this story mattered for Corinne. She spent two lessons on it too absorbed to listen to the tape, although that would have been easier. We believe strongly that this being the case, it would have been quite inappropriate for her teacher to respond negatively – either by commenting straightaway on the mistakes or by expressing disappointment that she had not used any information in her story about carboniferous forests. That may have been the teacher's intention but when, unpredictably, we tap an area of genuine concern to a child, perhaps we should be content to take note of it, not begrudge the fact that it's not what we were expecting.

Consider the possible effect that the teacher's written comment on our next piece might have had on the boy who produced it. We would suggest that like Corinne, Martin is possibly writing this story about himself; in some respects what the teacher has written would appear to confirm this . . .

The hunt   Martin (15–16)
A small fox was playing in the wood's with various odd's & end's that he found lying around when, he heard a sound that sent a chill's down his spine. It was the sound of dog's barking & he knew they were after him. So he started to run. but he had *Why* nowhere much to run to & not much time so he ran toward's the *the* *apostrophes?*

104

thick part of the wood that is more like a jungle than a wood. He ran as fast as his leg's would carry him, though the hounds were gaining on him but, he made it to the thick part of the wood which would help him, & slow the huntsmen & dog's down. He ran through bushe's, bramble's, pile's of leave's & hedge's, he leaped fellen tree's & pieces of rubbish left by stupid untidy picnicker's that had visited the wood's. He ran along tree trunks, & the narrowist of path's between tree's, through barbed wire and under gates but still he could hear that awful yapping of the hound's & the sound of horn's and shout's of huntsmen urging the dogs and horses to go faster. By now the little fox was beginning to get tired so he ran towards an old house where he knew there was a hole in the wall for him to hide in. He reached it and rushed into the house & hid in his hole. There he waited shaking & nearly frightened to death. He knew they would find him and kill him.

The hound's were getting closer & closer & he knew death was near, but then a funny thing happened, the sound of the hound's was getting further away. they weren't chasing him any more, or maybe they were chasing something else & not him. Anyway to him it didn't matter, it wasn't his turn to die.

I'm not v. impressed. Your work is mediocre lacking real control + care. You will force me to take the matter up with other staff unless you produce work of a higher quality

We noted earlier how re-shaping an experience in talk or writing often has the power to transmute events or feelings that were painful or disquieting when they were experienced directly, into a new experience which can bring a sense of satisfaction, even pleasure to the writer. All the children we have quoted so far in fact were looking back in some respects to such experiences, seeking to resolve more to their own satisfaction, moments when they had felt uncomfortable or ill at ease.

In the same way this next piece (which was in fact written in a Maths lesson) reflects an attempt by the writer to come to terms with an incident which has been disturbing him, by finding a shape for it. Again, like the others, it is still incomplete, still in the process of finding a form, as Adam reaches out for images that will convey his feelings adequately:

Funeral for a friend Adam (12–13)
Strange Divine
Death only takes time
7 bouquets of black
Dead Roses
Only Death takes the life out of living
7 feet underground
Rat's And worms eat you body away
Small crumpled Skin
Slim white cloth and tin (?)
the smile of Death is upon you
I'll see you at the
funeral for a friend.

When one of us talked to this boy about why he'd written a poem in one of his Maths lessons, he said at first that he just wasn't in the mood for doing Maths, but further discussion revealed that his mother, who worked in an old people's home, had been upset the previous weekend because she had had to help to lay out an old woman she had liked. Fortunately the boy's teacher, who was also his form tutor, was interested in him as well as in his Maths. She had enjoyed other poems that he had written and received this one with the same attention and appreciation.

Other people's lives

What Adam was exploring in *Funeral for a friend* was an experience that happened to his mother. Often when children set out to write poems and stories they choose to put out feelers into other people's lives, to discover what the world might look like through other eyes. All of us use language on occasions for this purpose, sometimes privately inside our own heads, sometimes in talk with friends and sometimes in writing. Here is another poem about death from a fifth year girl's CSE folder. In it she imagines what it might feel like for the dead person and for his relatives. We don't know what had put the thought of death into Sue's mind but writing this enabled her to try out the experience of bereavement. It's not just past experiences that can be re-created to our own satisfaction in poetic writing – possible future experiences can be equally compelling.

Death   Sue (15–16)

Nobody knows when death will come.
It can come like the wind stinging like a scorpion.
It can slowly grow like a weed that chokes,
until there is no life left in the body
and it gives way to permanent. (?)

Then relatives weep for the person who is gone.
They weep for their consciences that are filled with guilt.
They pray for a soul that has left them for ever,
and hope that their prayers will save them from punishment.

They wear black and try not to smile,
like children taking their punishment bravely,
but when the bell goes for home
they'll through off the mask of sorrow and go happy away.

The body lies waiting for decay to set in
and laughs at the foolish prayers
and the sorrow his relatives bring.

The body is happy it's sleeping in peace.
It has no more worries to trouble it now.
It need not be mourned over, it's only the living that can die,
he knows there is no more to come.

We suggested in the previous chapter that writing which focusses
on how people feel, can often reveal some implications of new
information more fully than a straight transactional report. We
quoted *A day in the workhouse* and *Grog* to show how imagined
reconstructions could illuminate the facts in this way. Here is one
further fairly typical example of how a knowledge of what happened
to someone else, at another time and in another place, can be
'realised' through the imagination of the writer. The girl who wrote
this had never been to the USA and never encountered a racially
divisive situation in her own school but she had read a long account
by a girl who had been one of the first nine black children to go to
Little Rock Central High School. She has already entered imagin-

atively into the situation as it was described by that girl; she now writes her own version of what it might have been like:

My first day at Little Rock Central Haidee (13–14)
I am a coloured girl, I am one of the nine children that have been moved from the all black school to Little Rock Central which had been all white.
It is September 5th, 1957. I am all tense and excited, yet I am fritened too. I feel so funny, I can't eat my breakfast. When I finished the little bit I had eaten I tried to read a book.
It was time to go. I didn't live far from the school so I walked. I got near to the school and saw crowds of people. Some of them were guards. When I appeared the crowds shouted 'Lynch her! Lynch her!' This scared me, but I felt safer when I thought of the guards. There was a great pushing around me. I began to feel faint. I walked towards the gate, the crowds shouted, 'Don't let her in, we don't want any niggers in our school'. I thought I was going to get in, but when I tried to push past them they wouldn't let me by. I didn't know what to do. The crowds shouting was deafening. I decided to walk. I wasn't going to let them know how scared I was. I walked past a lot of them, but I couldn't walk any more. I had to run. I ran all the way home. My mother was in the kitchen. She looked at me and trembled. She whispered 'Are you alright'
'Yes mum, I'm alright' I said.
'I'll never let you go to that school again.'
But I wanted to, I wanted to go to that school, but I wanted them to be friendly!

Other people's writing
Our next group of writings reflects the interweaving that can occur between reading other people's stories and poems and writing our own. We have been talking about how children find ways of projecting themselves imaginatively into other people's lives. They can do this by finding their own words – or they can make use of someone else's words; if the other person's writing is powerful enough, it can have the same impact on the reader as a 'real' ex-

perience and it is interesting to see what aspects of it they may then choose to take up in their own writing. Through Dylan Thomas's poem *Hunchback in the Park* Susan has caught a sense of loneliness and alienation which she re-creates in her own words. In Catherine's case, the poem *Hawk Roosting* by Ted Hughes, had been read to the whole class; many of the group have in that way been able to perceive the hawk (at any rate in their own terms), through the poet's eyes, and from the feelings and ideas excited by his writing and the pattern he has found for them, many have gone on to find a form of their own in which to re-work the experience for themselves.

The hunchback man   Susan (11–12)
He sits in the park and the boys and girls ridicule him. He has no new clothes, they are torn and old. He eats his food out of newspapers. His house is small and dirty. It is cold. He goes to the park where people are playing. He has no-one to keep him company. He is sad and lonely when he goes to the park. When it is night he goes to sleep in his house. It is uncomfortable. Bits of wood poking out of it. Dull. No-one likes him, they do not speak to him. He sits in the park until the bells ring, when the park closes. When the people ridicule him he tries not to take any notice

The kill   Catherine (12–13)
A shadow skims
across the undulating fields
like an arrow from a bow.

Rising, falling,
Curling wings round columns of air.
Eyes watching the ground.

Feeling the weather
Flowing through splayed-out feathers
Stimulating the circulation.

The grass moves below.
The face of an unsuspecting innocent
peeps out.

Sniffing the air
looking in all directions
Except above.

It is sighted.
The hawk tenses, excitement mounting
At the thought of the kill.
Now it's hovering
Waiting for the precise moment to drop
And attack.

NOW!

Like a speckled shooting star
He attacks.
Vicious claws
Rip fur, tear flesh from bones,
Blood staining the grass.

We came across *Runaway* in the Humanities notebook of a second year boy. It wove itself in and out of his other work and was still unfinished when we saw it. It was writing that he was doing from choice and with the motivation to continue it whenever he found the chance in between the pieces of written work that had been set by the teacher ('My house in the past – Roman Villa' and a comprehension exercise). At this stage it was already seven pages long. The plot is not unfamiliar: an orphaned boy who has been living with his aunt, running away with his trusty dog to fend for himself in the rough. Parts of it are strongly reminiscent of Jean George's novel *My Side of the Mountain* and when we asked Philip if he had read it, he said that he had and that he had enjoyed it very much. His own story (of which we only have space for an excerpt) is another clear illustration of how readers can become writers by entering into someone else's imaginary world and making it their own:

Runaway (an excerpt)   Philip (12–13)

He had stopped in the graveyard because it was quiet and no-one would look for him there. He didn't believe in ghosts but the trees were dripping as it had been raining all day but had stopped now the drips sounded like tiny footbeats. There was an owl hooting and this helped to scare Peter. He said 'ghosts who believes in them' and munched a slice of bread. When he had finished he had a drink of pop, then he went to sleep. He was woken by the dawn chorus as the book called it.

It was half past five by the church clock when Peter took to the road he thought he had another ten miles to go. He was going to a place called Hetcock Woods. He had been once with his father It was a big wood with plenty of wildlife to trap and eat there was a small river with plenty of fish in it.

He suddenly thought oh heck I need fish hooks and nylon so he bought some he now had £9.75. The only trouble was the shop-woman might recognise him if the police came round. He picked up some string I could do with some more string than the stuff I pick up off the ground. I can use nylon I suppose for nooses but I need string for tying things.

Peter got a lift to a village one mile before the woods and reached the wood by miday (he thought) he had reached the woods and walked in keeping well off the main paths. Telling Jip to be quiet he spotted a rabbit warren and after consulting his book he chose a well worn entry to the warren and set his trap he cut some nylon with his knife telling Jip to scat he put round the hole. He picked up his stick and waited. After 2 hours a rabbit came out and he pulled the noose and caught a rabbit he killed it with his stick. And letting Jip to guard it he went and gathered wood for a fire. He consulted his book and made a pyramid fire he lit it with 1 match feeling very proud and he went back and found Jip sitting over 2 dead rabbits one was bitten to death and the other he had killed with his stick. He skinned the rabbits and cooked them on a spit over the fire. He and Jip ate one and saved the other one for breakfast (he was going to have bread for tea).

'Phew I could do with a drink. Oh heck I haven't got anything to carry water in I must get a bottle to keep water in. Ah good I can hear water. He found the water it was a little spring. Up till then he hadn't thought about where he was going to live then started to worry he didn't fancy spending another night in the open. Then suddenly he saw 2 boulders lying 3 feet apart then he thought if I was to pull branches over those it wood be a perfect shelter water near by fairly near the river and the marshes where there were frogs this was one sort of food he knew he could get and near the forest in case people came looking for him which he hoped they wouldn't . . .

Making a construct with words

So far we have been concentrating on what children have chosen to write about when they set out to make a poem or a story. We have suggested that the focus of their attention will be on what the world looks like and feels like to the individual – drawing variously on their own experience and on the experience of others as they observe it or read about it. We now want to look more directly at how they discover and develop language patterns to shape these thoughts.

We know how from an early age children begin to experiment with the sound and intonational patterns that words can make when they are strung together – evolving distinctive rhythms, slipping easily to and fro from speech to song. So when they come to experimenting with written language, the roots for handling it artistically are already there in previous experiences with spoken language. Here is part of a transcript taken from a tape recording of two three-year-olds who were sitting on the living room window-sill, playing with a toy piano and a toy drum.

Stephen: The birds a play
　　　　　When the birds come out to play
　　　　　(The light?) went up the nothing
　　　　　(The light?) went up the nothing
　Kerry: . . . Stephen?
Stephen: (The light went) When the birds came out to play
　　　　　　　　　　　(Pause)
　　　　　　　　　　　The birds went up the drain spout.
　　　(singing)　　　Half a pound of tuppenny rice

Half a pound of treacle
Half a pound of tuppenny rice
Half a pound of treacle . . . in there
(And I know) Pop goes the weasel . . .
? . . . the weasel.

Kerry: (Plays toy piano)
Stephen: Pop goes the weasel! Herr! (Laughs)
Kerry: (Playing the piano) Can you sing Jack and Jill went up the hill to . . . ? . . . You do.
Stephen: Jack and Jill went up the hill
To fetch a pail of water
Kerry: and Jack fell down and broke his crown
You sing that as well now
Stephen: An eagle, an eagle he woke – an eagle . . .
Kerry: Now . . . Jack and Jill went up the hill (much vigorous piano playing)
Stephen: Now Jack and Jill went up the hill . . .
Kerry: Not yet! Not yet! . . . Play.
Stephen: Eh, don't keep doing that – don't make those tunes like that! Just go: (banging on drum) I'll show you.
Kerry: Not yet!

Part of what Stephen and Kerry are doing here is playing with the form of nursery rhymes that they know – experimenting with word changes and rhythm changes in a way that satisfies and amuses them. In much the same way, older children can gain an aesthetic pleasure from playing with form, sometimes lightheartedly, sometimes with the seriousness of a professional artist. In schools, it is probably English teachers again who will be most familiar with this kind of trying-it-out poetic writing where the attention is focussed predominantly on the shape – where it is the medium which is most engaging the writer's attention, exciting or intriguing him. *Tantalus* seems to us to reflect this kind of engagement; the writer is taking pleasure in weaving a tapestry of words to produce what is in effect, a set piece, to be admired chiefly for its decorative qualities.

Tantalus   Claire (11–12)
Neck deep
in a watery wilderness,
starving –
parching –
pleading –
I live on.
Before me dangle
succulent
round
juicy grapes
which, when I grasp
slither out of reach
like the slippery clasp of a fish

The recognition that it is fun to play with words can contribute to the enjoyment of both writer and reader – witness the popularity of Spike Milligan's poetry across a wide age range. Here are some contributions (from a first year group in a secondary school) which were all voluntary, about a hairy caterpillar that the class had been studying in biology. After the first verse had been pinned on the classroom noticeboard, a whole collection of other verses and drawings follows. Here are some of them:

How horrid is mummy
How nasty is she:
She called Wilbur a maggot
When she had him for tea.

Wilbur washed his hair last night
And put it in a plait.
This morning he's so fuzzy,
That he looks quite round and fat.

Wilbur washed his hair last night
Before he went to bed,
Because it got into his eyes,

In his ears and up his nose,
And even in between his toes,
That nasty, greasy, matted fuzz.
(It still does.)

Wilbur's football crazy,
He kicks a ball all day
And he supports old Arsenal
In his caterpillar way!!

One of the attractions of the poetic function is the freedom that it gives to both writer and reader to take on the role of a spectator: to daydream, reflect, contemplate, without the pressure to *do* anything about it. In a paper on the subject, James Britton (Britton and Newsome 1968) points out that:

> When we take up this role, then we are freed from certain responsibilities and we use this freedom to do other things: in particular we attend to the utterance itself as a form or as a set of forms. We attend to the form of the language, its sounds and rhythms, to the pattern of events in a story and to the pattern of feelings embodied – the changing kaleidoscope of tension and relief, fear and hope, love and hate. When we are *participating* in actual affairs, feelings tend to be sparked off in action: as spectators, we are able to savour feeling and perceive the form it takes.

We have tried to describe in this chapter how the writing research model enables us to trace how children develop the ability in their own writing 'to savour feeling and perceive the form it takes'. One of the most useful features of this way of analysing the growth of writing ability is that it is able to avoid such evaluative distinctions as true/false, good/bad, first rate/second rate. Alternatively, the spectrum of writing functions makes it possible to trace writing on the move from the intimate sharing which requires a known and trusted listener or reader, to an offered communication (transactional or poetic), which is meaningful because the writer's handling of language makes it so.

We would like to include at this point a few such pieces which are dominantly poetic in function. They are written by children of various ages, some of them voluntarily, others arising out of a context created by a teacher. Some reflect a response to the outside world, some a response to the inner world of private feelings; some draw more obviously than others on the work of other writers. What we believe they share in a sense, is an independence of such auto-biographical contexts, because for each of these writers there was a moment when their feelings flowed strongly into words; these words shaped a facet of their experience in such a way that it still continues of its own accord to catch the light.

We are not suggesting that an end point has been reached, a 'goal' arrived at in the sense that from now on whenever these writers try to express their feelings, perfect poems and stories will flow from them. More often than not it will continue to be a struggle to shape experience as perceptively as this, but for whatever reasons, on this occasion they found the words they wanted.

The Christmas tree　　　　　　　　　　　　　Maurice (10–11)
Its branches are twisted and thick
Its lights shine in the night sky.
The moon is dull against the lights of the tree.
The branches are streamlined.
The curved trunk extended into the air.
Pine needles sharp as knives
The trunk is gnarled and bumpy.
The silver balls are shining as the moonlight catches them.
The great red pot sits under the shaggy tree.
It is weighed down with decorations.

The pike　　　　　　　　　　　　　　　　　　Steve (14–15)
The float screeched away,
Suddenly the float had gone.
I let out some line,
An illusion of freedom,
Then I struck hard,
Burying the hook deep into its jaws,

The pike was on.
The fight went on
Hopefully but not yet won.
Each run
I held
And wearing him down
Reeled him in,
The net under him
Finally secure
I felt relief and joy.
Taking him from the net
His gaze and mine met,
His unblinking eyes say
Another day, another day.

The orchard   Paul (16–17)
When once
In this summer field
The ground was wet with heat
And the trees hung too heavy with fruit
A knight rode up
Drew his blade
And sliced off t
                    h
                      e
                        h
                          e
                            a
                              d
                                   of the farmer
And his daughter
Who had been picking apples
Lazily.

And now their heads lay
                          apart
                          from
                          their
                          bodies

Gazing upward through green branches
Their eyes were open
And dropping fruit rotted beside them.

The mad knight rode off
Slashing at the boughs above his head
Bringing apples bouncing and bruising behind him
And he and his laughter disappeared
Leaving heads and apples
Rotting together.

Intrusion into a head   Janice (17–18)

A small hut stood in the heart of a wood. Inside, the furniture
consisted of two cupboards, a table with drawers, and various
sized cardboard boxes. A small fire flickered in one corner of the
room. The fire never quite died, although it never seemed to be
fed with fuel. Outside the hut the wind blew and rain knocked
on the two barred windows. There was a door in the hut, but
very few people ever entered through it. The place had been
deserted for a long time, and its only visitors were passers by,
who stopped to peep in through the windows and wandered
away again, never thinking of it further.
One of these people stumbled upon the hut on a particularly
stormy day. The hut looked even smaller and more desolate
than ever before from the outside. The stranger was soaked by
the rain and decided to enter the hut. He knocked at the door,
but no-one answered it. He called out to anyone who may have
missed the knock, and the hut seemed to groan a little, but no-
one answered. The stranger peered in through one of the
windows, which had bars up at it. But he still saw no-one. The
fire made him think that the occupant was inside, but probably
asleep, and unable to hear him. He tapped on the glass and
called again, but still there was no reply. The rain fell heavily
again, and felt even more bitter. So the stranger returned to the
door and tried the handle. But it was locked. He knocked again,
but there was still no reply. In his desperation he forced the
lock and even then something seemed to be pushing the door
shut again. It took a great effort to open it, and when he even-

tually got in, it seemed as if someone had been pushing it and had suddenly moved away. The stranger fell onto the floor, where he stayed for a while.

Although the small fire still flickered in one corner of the room, the inside of the hut felt cold. The stranger climbed to his feet, and fastened the top button of his shirt. He sat down on a small box, which immediately collapsed, leaving the stranger in a helpless mess on the floor, among sheets of paper. Slightly angered by this, he staggered to his feet again, and kicked the remains of the box across the room. Again he tried to sit down. He was successful this time. He sat close to the fire, which still refused to give out but the tiniest amount of warmth. Just as he had begun to doze, he was startled by a piece of paper which fluttered by. At first he thought a draught had caused this and looked around for a possible inlet. But no draught existed in the room. Such a refreshing element would never be allowed to enter this place. There was only the cold he had felt when he first came into the hut.

Again he sat down by the fire, but before he had closed his eyes, a loud groan had filled the room. He looked about the room, but saw nothing that could have released such a painful and tormented sound. The hut was silent again and the rain had turned into sleet outside, which battered fiercely against the barred windows.

The stranger felt too uncertain and uncomfortable to sleep now. He sat for a while staring about the room. Then he picked up one of the sheets of paper from the box he had kicked across the room. He intended to just glance at it to occupy himself as he felt aware of someone watching him. But what he saw on the paper almost seemed to jump at his throat and to throttle him. It was an account of someone's thoughts written down, as they had occurred to that someone. The thoughts were not in carefully organised sentences but just groups of words. Each group of words seemed immediately to form an ugly, distorted picture. The stranger picked up another piece of paper. This was very similar but it also contained a few simple thoughts which seemed pleasant compared with the others. He looked into the drawer in the table. There were more sheets of paper. These were even more simple and bearable to the stranger. He gradually made his way through those in the drawers and started on those in the boxes. Some contained very little out of the ordinary while others told of events, fantasies and thoughts which were too perverted in the stranger's eyes. Some of the grotesque images trapped in these words seemed to fling themselves from the paper. In one corner of the room a man who the stranger recognised as himself, stood, chopping with his own bare hand into the skull of a child writhing at his feet. In another part of the room, another image of himself was hacking into the chest of another child, with his bare hand.

The stranger covered his eyes and stood before these scenes. He took his hands away for a moment, hoping they would be gone. But they were still there, becoming even more bloody. Eventually the stranger was able to move. He turned towards the door, but the scenes appeared before him still. He fell on his knees and screamed continuously. The faces of the battered children turned towards him and smiled. Their smiles were not the smiles of children but ones that distorted their faces so as to make them look like old men.

The images of himself still continued their destruction, but it seemed to the stranger that every blow to the children was being done to himself. He felt his heart being wrenched from his chest by his own hand. He felt his hand squeezing all of the emotion he had ever had from his heart. His other hand sank into his skull and pounded down every fantasy he had ever had. The scenes from the paper were now enveloped in himself.

The fire that had flickered in the corner suddenly grew larger and hotter. It reached out towards the body of the stranger and took him into itself. As it did this, it screeched out a horrible laugh, then sank back into the corner. The hut was left alone again, to decay.

As children learn to use language which is transactional in function, they will learn how to shape their thoughts with increasing explicitness and precision. The focus of their attention will be on the world as it exists outside themselves and their efforts will be directed towards understanding how it works as exactly and accurately as they can. Knowledge in this context may have important personal implications for both writer and reader and may personally affect the decisions of each but it will not be *centred* in the unique shapes that experiences take on for individuals.

As children learn to use language (particularly written language) which is poetic in function, they will discover that in this domain those areas of learning and perception which are centred in the self are of supreme importance. What is being offered by writer to reader is above all a view of reality as he sees it – and as it matters to him. The lens in the poetic is closer to a human eye than a microscope – it is a subjective look at the world, coloured by the experiences, thoughts and feelings of a particular person and valued for that reason.

The move out of an expressive use of language in either direction, towards the poetic or towards the transactional, involves a heightened degree of organising thought and shaping it. But the direction taken will deeply affect the nature of that organisation. In the transactional function the emphasis is towards a linear, logical set of connections – an inductive or deductive hierarchy of points. In the poetic function, as Langer especially has shown, the patterning is non-discursive; the connections are implicit and themselves provide the structure which renders the whole inseparable from the parts.

Each function offers different possibilities of knowing which can be tremendously valuable to the learner. By approaching what is new and unfamiliar from different angles, each allows for its own insights. What we should seek to avoid is an overstructured approach to knowledge in schools, where the signposts in each subject on the timetable only point in one direction.

References

BRITTON, J. and NEWSOME, B. (1968) What is learnt in English lessons? *Journal of Curriculum Studies* 1, 1, November

LANGER, S.K. (1953) *Feeling and Form* Routledge and Kegan Paul

Chapter five

What is emerging

In this chapter we try to interpret the outcome of our four years' work with teachers. The book, as a whole, is chiefly concerned to document and explore in its practical outcomes a view of language and learning derived from the writing research. The examples of children's written and spoken language have come from individuals or small groups of teachers who were interested in the research and made use of it. They do not generally represent the work of whole schools. Can we, therefore, say anything *general* about what seems to be emerging? We think we can, although our work is not wide enough, or representative enough, for our interpretation to be more than tentative. Furthermore, not all the teachers who have worked with us would interpret the outcomes in the same way as we do – though some would. It is also important to remember that many teachers who have never heard of the writing research or the Project are themselves operating in similar ways. In any development project there are hundreds of people who are at this point or that point and who could feed into it if you could only get hold of them and who, in many cases, are feeding into their own circles of local research and activity. So what we have probably been doing is focussing and hastening some current trends and inhibiting others. We do not want to underestimate the value of this because it is important to see these changes against a background of theory and research so that they need not be regarded as merely the pendulum swing of fashion.

When we began in 1971 we saw the problem as the altering of people's view of language. In general, people either think of language as something to be corrected and improved, or they take it for granted and just use it. Our aims at first were to get people to recognise it as a major intellectual tool. We now think this doesn't go far enough. We found that 'wrong' language policies can prevent learning but 'right' language policies don't necessarily *produce* learning. We began to suspect that when we found the kinds of writing we were looking for they were, in a sense, 'exceptions', or isolated examples. Working from this hypothesis we gradually shifted the focus of our attention from how people view language to how they view learning, and we used selected written utterances as points of departure for an analysis of the situations from which they came. We tried to determine what the enabling – or disabling – features for learning of these situations were and what part language was playing in the whole complex. The first four chapters give our account of this work.

School situations are not laboratory situations, and attempts to treat them as such are likely to produce false results. Every piece of writing, and the circumstances that gave rise to it, represents a network of past experience, relationships and expectations linked to a continuum of other such networks. In this chapter we attempt to identify what are emerging for us as the most significant features in these webs of learning and language, and also to identify what seem to be the knottiest problems. But, as might be expected, the items which we see as significant are themselves a network. This interrelatedness throws light on why efforts by individual teachers to make a change here or a change there have only resulted in what we have referred to as 'isolated cases' of progress. Changes have to be more widespreading to be effective.

How a learner sees himself

It seems to us the most influential factor in school learning is how a learner sees himself in relation to the various things he does at school. Does he see reading, writing, doing experiments, giving talks, answering in class, or not doing any of these things, as belonging to the kind of person he thinks he is? But his view of himself as a school student largely depends on how his teachers see him, and how he interprets his position in the various competitive hierarchies of school – fast or slow learner, sport teams, popularity, physique, exam results etc.

How his teacher sees him – and responds to his efforts or lack of effort – depends in turn upon how the teacher sees *himself*. Does he see himself as someone who is in some sort of senior partnership relation to his pupils or a figure of unquestionable authority by virtue of his role? His view of his role as a teacher is, of course, closely related to his view of learning. Thus, out of this mutually dependent teaching-learning relationship children see themselves as, and sometimes become, partners, friends, enemies, rebels, independent thinkers, students, readers, writers, doers of experiments etc. When we look at language in these contexts we find that the kind of language and the kind of experience which is reckoned appropriate to the classroom scene is closely related to the teacher's view of learning and his role relationships to his pupils (see Roger Lewis's illuminating article in *English in Education*).

We quote in illustration from a letter we received from a teacher in a comprehensive school. She sent us some writings by her pupils, one of which had been school printed as a pamphlet called *The magic marble*. She wrote: *The magic marble* is a breakthrough story by a twelve year old boy who had been very withdrawn and rather friendless. He wrote very little and with many mistakes. We were writing "novels" in his class and he wrote six lines.'

The magic marble   Colin (12)
Chapter 1.
My name was Joe and I went to St Georges School in Ealing. One Friday I was walking along slowly when I saw a marble. I picked it up and rubbed it. Then I put it in my pocket and started to walk along South Street where I saw my cousin Jenny. I called her. She looked around. I called again, she stopped to wait for me.

His teacher continued: 'Somehow I responded correctly and he did chapter 2 – ten lines – and then proceeded to chapter 3 and chapter 4 till the book was finished at chapter 21. Each chapter was written on a new page. He was very shy about it and the whole thing took about five weeks. Since a story implies an audience I read it to the class who were most impressed. Then his father rang the school to say that Colin seemed very happy recently and thanked us. Since this he's been writing well and after discussion about getting speech down on paper his writing is now almost correct, and this applies to his spelling too. Now that his story has been "printed" as a pamphlet it's been used very successfully with pupils in remedial withdrawal classes. I gave it to a little West Indian boy called Peter for halfterm and he came back after the holiday raving to "write" his own. This is now on tape waiting to be transcribed.'

Many teachers, of course, have experience of this kind of break-through, but we chose this one because Colin's teacher made it so clear that what was afoot was the writing of real stories, not school exercises. She assumed that stories are written to be read, or listened to, so the class was the first audience, as of course it often is, but she didn't stop there. It was typed and duplicated with a coloured cover on pamphlet-sized paper and read in another class – a class of slow readers. The way the teachers treated Colin's story made reading and writing stories a possibility for these children too. The language of Colin's story is very like written-down speech and captures details of his life and feelings, and it was carefully revised by Colin because it was for others to read.

We know of other schools where the stories (and poems) written by the children are reproduced as booklets, and are used in some classes because they often do for slow readers just what Colin's story did – bring reading and writing into the children's view of what they themselves do, that is they begin to see themselves as readers and writers. But it is not only the slow readers who enjoy these booklets. They are often sold at a few pence in the school, and to parents, and are widely enjoyed.

One further comment: Colin's teacher said that his writing was now almost correct and that applied to his spelling too. In short, if you are writing a real book which people are going to read you want it to be correct in all its typographical details, so there is a real incentive for correct spelling and punctuation. What does all this add up to? At one time it might be supposed that it could have been summed up in the traditional school report remark: 'Colin has made good progress in his written work.' We think this kind of remark obscures the real things that have been happening. Colin's view of himself was altered by writing this 'book'; altered so markedly that his parents reported the change to his school, but they reported it in terms of his happiness. But this was not all. He had tasted, if only momentarily, the 'literary tradition' which is part of all our lives and which assumes readers. A real readership with its attendant usefulness and pleasure came into sight. Other children's views of themselves were changed too.

Our next example comes from a fourth year boy of thirteen from a large comprehensive school. One of our project officers was interested in the volume of work in his file, talked to him about it and asked him to write something about his writings. What follows is what he typed himself. We include excerpts from it here because we think it illuminates the crucial significance of how a learner views himself. Steve sees himself as a student – a learner – and he sees writing as an important aid to him. He comments on how he learns and he reflects on his own progress, and this self-imposed task of reflecting on his various writings causes him to make critical comments about some of his pieces. It is also interesting to see the distinction he makes between the tasks which he selected for quite expedient reasons from worksheets and those which sprang from his own interests. We have not printed the writings themselves because at this point in the chapter it is the writer's view of himself that we are attending to, and such an explicit account of his view of his work and of himself as a learner is rare in a student of thirteen.

Why I write what I write   Steve (13)
For each of the following pieces of work I have given an account of why I actually wrote them and why I wrote them in the way I did.

The pieces of work are:
Prisons.
The Cutteslowe walls.
The Suffragettes.
A report on the students demonstration in Leicester on October 31 1973.
The French involvement in Vietnam.*
The American involvement in Vietnam.*
The British political system.
The case for UFOs.
The Ultraterristrials.
(*These pieces of work are connected with, though are not a part of, a project on the whole history of Vietnam. The piece of

work on the demonstration is part of a project on protests which is not yet complete; however, it does not require the rest of the project to make sense.)

Prisons
This piece of work was to be honest just done because there happened to be a worksheet on prisons available. It is not part of a project and was really to fill in time while I was not working on a project. I very rarely work from worksheets as I like to gather my information from books etc and do 'my thing' rather than the ideas on the worksheet. However this worksheet had suggestions which coincided with my ideas and it had the information necessary to write these ideas. Though this could not be done in detail without more information, but as I said this was not intended to be done in detail but to fill in time. I find some of the worksheets very useful to do a short piece of work while I have nothing else to do, as they put a lot of information in a very compact form and in very small detail.

This particular piece of work I did for two reasons, it was my opinion the most interesting worksheet available at the time and I have views against the prison service as it stands at the moment. Although these reasons exist I cannot say that I would have done this piece of work if I did not happen to have a lesson with nothing else to do.

This piece of work or any other has not been done really for the teacher. This I can easily say but what is the reason? This is much harder to answer. I think one of the reasons is that I enjoy writing these things because it clears my mind to some extent what my views in whatever the subject is. It also teaches me a lot about the subject – which does teach you to keep your mouth shut when you think you know it all already. I have started pieces of work thinking that I knew it all and then finding that I knew nothing about it. So it does teach you, me at any rate, that however much you think you know about a subject there is still a lot more to know. The same thing occurs when I come back to a piece of work I have already done to use for something else or to improve it – I find there is a lot more to the subject than I ever knew about however much work I have done on it. So therefore every piece of work becomes a shot with a target being something that I cannot improve if I go back to it in two months six months or whatever. This is a target I will never achieve but I do feel I get nearer to it with every project and piece of work.

Another thing about the work on prisons is that it is not just a straightforward account of a prison but does contain some of my ideas. So the work also becomes a vehicle for getting my views across to someone else, where if they are not agreed with they will not come in for the attacking that views disagreed with normally would.

We note his recognition that there are patches of time in school that have to be filled in 'as best you can', but he can turn even these to good account: 'I find some of the worksheets very useful to do a short piece of work while I have nothing else to do, as they put a lot of information in a very compact form . . .'.

We wonder, do other school students also see worksheets as time-fillers? We note too the value that he places on his own ideas, choice of topic and methods of using resources. This is a dominant thread in his comments on his work.

> . . . I very rarely work from worksheets as I like to gather my information from books etc and do 'my thing' rather than the ideas on the worksheet. However this worksheet had suggestions which coincided with my ideas. . . . (and) . . . Another thing about the work on prisons is that it is not just a straightforward account of a prison but does contain some of my ideas.

We would also want to draw attention to the way he assesses his own work:

> . . . I have started pieces of work thinking that I knew it all and then finding that I knew nothing about it. . . . The same thing occurs when I come back to a piece of work I have already done to use it for something else or to improve it. . . . So therefore

every piece of work becomes a shot with a target being something that I cannot improve if I go back to it in two months six months or whatever. This is a target I will never achieve but I do feel I get nearer to it with every project and piece of work.

And in his account of his work on 'The student's demo' he writes:

I realise now having done this piece of work that it is really very bad. This is one of the reasons I would like to do more work in this way (writing from first-hand information) – to try to reach my unobtainable target.

And of his project on 'The British political system' he says:

This was the first big project I did and now when I look at it I marvel at how pathetic it is . . . I have placed emphasis on the wrong things and made all the mistakes I was warned about . . . so it ended up in my eyes a great failure. But I have learnt more from that project than any other piece of work I have ever done at school so it was only a failure in terms of what it was, not what was learnt from it. I learnt not only how to improve my work from this project but believe it or not I also learnt a great deal more than I already knew about the British political system although most of it is not in the project.

It needs to be said that Steve came from a school where the students work independently through projects, special studies and worksheets. Moreover, the confidence with which he assesses his position as a learner implies a partnership relation with his teachers.

In chapter one we have quoted a comparable report on a chemistry project for his CSE folder by a fifth form boy, together with his teacher's comment: '. . . throughout there is evidence of clear scientific thinking in Nigel's own words', and we quote again from Nigel's project ('On getting alcohol from paper') because it seems to us that in the way he has written up his experiments and in his final page comments (p.28) we can recognise a student (of no special ability) who nevertheless sees himself as a competent learner who can use the resources of a lab, make use of books, have success and failure and know what he needs to know to proceed further. He sees himself as comfortable in the world of enquiry. We would suggest that chiefly he sees himself in this way because this is the view his teacher has of him. We quote the last paragraph of his account of his last experiment to illustrate our comments and his teacher's. Nigel was at the same school as Steve.

I tasted the alcohol by putting my finger in the alcohol and then putting it on my tongue, it tasted of yeast and left a dry taste in my mouth.

After testing the alcohol I tried to burn it without much success. I put one or two on some rocksell wool but all that happened was the rocksell wool burnt from the heat of the Bunsen. So I tried it again but lighting it with a splint, but all that happened was that the splint burnt away. But I still had a few drops of alcohol left so I put one or two on some cotton wool and the same thing happened again. When that happened I came to the conclusion it was yeast so I dipped some cotton wool in some water which had yeast dissolved in it, then tried to burn it and nothing happened but I've not got enough proof to say it was the yeast.

We conclude this section on how the learner sees himself by an example which shows the other side of the coin. Here is a student who sees himself as someone who can't write adequately and who can't think for himself. He has some confidence in his capacity to understand what he is taught but none in his capacity to use language in a way that is acceptable to his teachers. He must partly have acquired this view of himself from the way his teachers have responded to his work.

Ian was studying A level English and History in the lower sixth.

We quote some of the things he said in a conversation with one of the project officers.

I *understand* it all, it's just my way of expressing it – I couldn't express myself, not in the way they told us to express it . . . .

You can make notes in your own way, except when you come to an exam – you've got to look at it and you've got to change it. If there was someone who could understand how I wrote and he was an examiner, then I'd like it much better. . . .

I'm always thinking of writing in their style . . . you're thinking so much of writing in their style that you're not really thinking what you're writing about. . . .

I suppose you think them (teachers) to be more intelligent, so you try and, you know, catch up with them I suppose – try and be equal – and you know it's not possible so you don't want to say anything. . . .

I'd like to write in a nice style so that everybody could understand it, but I can't find that possible. . . .

When we asked Ian if he would write something for us in his own way, he replied: 'I wouldn't think that was possible now after studying the texts that I have studied, because I've been influenced by the other teachers – they've influenced me, I don't think I could think for myself.'

In our view, Ian's salvation could only lie in his being encouraged to express his own thinking in his own language, the validity and quality of this being accepted by his teachers. Given this, his sixth-form texts, and *open* discussions about them with his peers and teachers, might gradually enlarge his language resources and change his view of himself.

Ian's comments about his work are in striking contrast to Nigel's, yet it is possible that some teachers might have regarded Nigel's language as inappropriate for a science report in spite of evidence of 'clear scientific thinking throughout'. This is a tangled knot to unravel and we discuss the role of a student's own language in learning more fully in *The role of everyday language in learning: some of the problems* (p. 143).

A writer's sense of audience

Most school writing is initiated by the teacher so the teacher is the ostensible audience, directly or indirectly, but the process of writing is more complicated than that. The monitoring self is always a part of a writer's sense of audience, as well as those others – the class, friends, examiners sometimes, parents perhaps, and a shadowy 'public' – who lurk behind his shoulder. The three written utterances quoted above were initiated by teachers but it seems to us Steve was writing very much for himself as well – getting things clear for himself – compare also Ian in his conversation. Colin's story had his own class as part of his conscious audience, though stories, if they are any good, are always more rooted in the writer's self than consciously built to an audience. In speech the actual or potential feedback from the listener continuously modifies what is said because the audience is physically present – right there in front of you – and sooner or later will speak too and thereby modify what you say next. In writing there is no such feedback. The actual audience, normally, slips away into the background leaving the writer free to pursue the meanings he wants to get down on paper. But somewhere, out of the direct focus of attention, a sense of an audience remains, ready to take shape when summoned, or stepping forward uncalled, as Ian described earlier in this chapter. We think it likely that one reason for the great amount of inert, inept writing produced by school students is that the natural process of internalising the sense of an audience, learned through speech, has been perverted by the use of writing as a testing or reproductive procedure at the expense of all other kinds of writing. When a writer's focus is on returning as exactly as possible what he has been given, the sense of any other audience, including the monitoring, reflective, independent self, disappears, leaving incomprehension, resentment or despair, or alternatively the satisfaction of producing something to satisfy someone else's demands. We think the following conversation throws light on some of these matters.

Andrew (a third year boy) is talking to one of the project officers who knows his school and his teachers well. They are talking about Andrew's humanities project on 'The industries and populations of towns' and are referring to an anecdote he had included about slavery:

BN: There's an anecdote about a grave . . . it was something about slaves – it was something about, er, in a cemetery near Harlow there's a gravestone which says on it 'Here lies so-and-so, the property of somebody-or-other' . . . How did you find that out?

A: Well, we just moved – 'cos we don't live far from that end, we'll go to church fairly often, and, we went round to see that church 'cos we saw it from the road and I like looking at gravestones and that and I saw it and it sort of fitted in with that.

BN: And who are you asking the question of 'Rather unusual to put on a grave, don't you think?'

A: Well, that's to anyone who reads it.

BN: Do you think of your reader?

A: Yea.

BN: Who do you think of?

A: Anyone who reads it. Mainly Sir, 'cos he reads it. And anyone else.

BN: But I mean, when you put a thing like that, or your jokes, do you think to yourself 'How will Mr S . . . react' or do you think in more general terms, how will anybody react – you know?

A: More general, I think, how would anyone.

BN: You do? So you're not just thinking of him.

A: Oh, no.

BN: Would you, I mean, it's kind of a bit odd because you say that mostly these just get stockpiled, you know, so they're not read by anyone else normally.

A: Not really, no. But we're always told to write it as though we're trying to explain to someone else of our own age – so we just get used to it.

BN: So you do it, I mean you do actually think of other people reading it even though you don't expect them ever to do it?

A: Yea, that's how we have to. They always write out 'as if to someone of your same age', and you've got to tell them about it.

. . . .

BN: In some of these things you give your opinions, don't you?

A: Oh, yea, most of it.

BN: You like giving your opinions, do you?

A: Yea.

BN: Do you very often get asked for them?

A: Mostly, yea. Especially in this subject. (Some talk about the humanities projects of the class.)

BN: It looked to me as though you were looking for the chance to give your view.

A: Well, perhaps, yea . . .

BN: This is a bit you wrote about *To Sir, With Love*, you said 'On reading this section from the book . . . I felt thoroughly annoyed to think that those businessmen wanted a man for the job but when they found that he was coloured, they rejected him and what was more annoying was that those men probably gave the position to a less intelligent white man.' That was just how you began. So already you're expressing an attitude – you're saying what you think about it.

A: Yea. I don't think we were asked to put our opinion on that but I was annoyed. When I usually do something, I always position myself as the person like now, I mean I was treating myself as the coon who got turned down.

It seems that Andrew, in his writing, takes account both of his actual audience – his teacher – and some potential wider audience. Earlier in this conversation he had said that he often puts jokes in his writing because his teacher enjoys them and he himself likes them. This seems near to a trusted adult audience, which we think the most fruitful in developing writing ability because it allows a writer to experiment with safety. Andrew also understands the convention which requires him to write *as if for* some particular audience – 'they always write out "as if to someone of your same age", and you've got to tell them about it'; and he understands that this convention allows him to express his own opinions and feelings within the framework of the 'as if' situation. He says, 'I always position myself as the person, like now, I mean I was treating myself as the coon who got turned down.'

We have found an increasing number of teachers who have tried to create situations involving an audience other than themselves – real or imagined – as a context for the writing they have asked their pupils to do. On the whole this tends to come from teachers concerned with the humanities. In the sciences and among older students there is perhaps an unspoken sense that this is a device for younger children or for less serious studies, yet the American psychologist George Kelly in a paper called 'The language of hypothesis' describes an attitude and a corresponding use of language which would help to bridge the gap between the known and the unknown – which, of course, is just what teachers are trying to do when they ask children to write 'as if they were . . .' or 'what would happen if . . .'; Kelly calls this the use of the invitational mood. He says that at moments of risk we would be greatly helped if we deliberately abandoned the indicative mood and operated in the invitational mood with its language form, 'let us suppose . . .'. He says that this procedure suggests that things are open to a wide range of constructions and 'there is something in stating a new outlook in the form of a hypothesis that leaves the person himself intact and whole'. When students reflect on their work or even report what they know, they put themselves at risk in terms of their teacher audience, or any audience for that matter, and we would stress the value of the invitational mood both with regard to a hypothetical audience as well as hypothetical ideas. We have included a number of writings which we think illustrate the usefulness of these hypothetical situations in chapter three ('My first day in the workhouse', 'Grog', 'School revolution' and 'The X machine'). We quote one further example here because the 'as if' situation is directly one of audience, 'Suppose you wanted to explain what diffusion is to a younger child who has not done any science and does not know what molecules are':

Explaining diffusion   Frances (14)
We all know that gases are invisible, in other words we can't

see it there but it is present. Gases are made up of molecules, for the moment let us call molecules 'marbles'. These marbles are present in solids as well, but here they are squeezed together and are unable to move. But in a gas the marbles (which cannot be seen with the human eye, only with an electronic microscope) move about freely and do not move in one specific direction, they move at random. . . .

Gillian (13)

Molecules are small blobs which are found in you, me, blocks of ice and in fact everything. They are very tiny and can't be seen by the naked eye. There are millions of molecules and they all join up to form an object. . . . .

This, of course, was an 'exercise', but it was also a game played by the children and the teacher – a combined knowledge and language game. The pupils had to manipulate their knowledge and their language to serve an audience other than themselves and their teacher, and as their teacher observed you only really understand ideas like these when you can play with them – suppose this, and suppose that, in Kelly's terms.

Our next examples come from situations where the writing was directed to real audiences other than the teacher. First, the *Cleveland Evening Gazette*. The English adviser arranged for the paper to carry a weekly feature page, 'Report from the Cleveland classrooms'. A different school would be responsible for the page each week. This feature would run for six or seven weeks, and then be picked up again later in the year if it interested the readers. There is far too much matter to include here, so we print the editorial paragraphs which head three of these weekly feature pages.

February 20th

Today we introduce a new *Evening Gazette* weekly feature – 'Report from the Cleveland classrooms'. This page is written by Overfields Junior School, Ormesby, who visited the Hexham area with Ian Richmond to see how the old lead miners lived and worked. The stories set the general scene, tell the legend of the haunted mine, describe Carr's Cave, life in a lodging shop, and how children were used to scrape lead from the flue tunnel. The reports are as the children wrote them – well almost. We have tidied up some of the grammar and spelling without, we hope, losing the freshness and simplicity of approach.

There are photographs of the classroom exhibition, headlines in varying size type, the pieces are signed, and there is a wide range of kinds of writing: stories – 'The volunteer who was never seen again', and 'Spooks in the dark'; a report – 'How we started on top of England'; two poems – '. . . because the lead mine monster lurked!' and 'Down into the damp, dark tunnel'; and an imagined reconstruction of living in a lodging shop.

February 27th
Pupils of Warsett School, Brotton have written our second report from the Cleveland classrooms. They tell how the school helps spastic children, and describe some of the things going on in the neighbourhood. The pictures were taken by Al Coleman. Next week: 'Norton Glebe Junior School looks at the First World War'.

March 13th
Pupils of Marton Sixth Form College, Middlesborough, make today's report from the Cleveland classrooms. The college has, until 1976, pupils of under sixth form age and some of the work is produced by pupils in their fourth or fifth year. The work covers several subjects, but broadly reflects the pupils' interests in their own environment and Cleveland county, and its surroundings.

As with the pages contributed by the younger children, this page carries reports, a story – 'What a north-east town might be like when the iron and oil had run out' – opinions and a poem:

Continuously, monotonously,
the tall concrete towers
Churn out clouds of never ending smog.
As time goes by,
Slowly the whole landscape
will become engulfed by a
network of structural steel,
While beneath this mechanical mass
Life still goes on.
Life without aim,
Life without meaning,
Just one repetitive day after day.
Each morning, men of all ages,
Hurry to their industrial employment.

Karen Robson

We conclude this section with two accounts of a visit to the
London Transport Museum by fourth year girls. The second
clearly shows the effect on writing that a specific audience can have
even when the writing is only a straightforward task of reporting.
The first piece is a completely routine report of a school activity,
reflecting the teacher's instructions in the heading 'Things we
noticed', and is partly in note form. The second piece was written
by Sandra and Deborah for a magazine from their school for one of
their 'feeder' junior schools. The sense of an audience of junior
school children has obviously influenced the writing of the second
piece. They felt the stories had to be really well presented, i.e. there
was an audience to be reckoned with here.

A visit to Syon Park   Jaqueline (14)
On January 23rd Deborah C., Sandra S., Josette C. and I all
went to Syon Park's London Transport Museum.
  We caught a 217a bus to Waltham Cross, then a 715 green
line bus that took us to Hammersmith. At Hammersmith we
caught a red bus 204 to Syon Park.
  The London Transport Museum was in a fairly large garage-

type-Hall, inside the old buses were spaced out nicely in lines, there was also items of interest e.g. old newspaper cuttings, models of old buses etc. in a glass cabinet. You could also buy picture postcards of the buses with information on the back.

Things we noticed

1 The first thing we noticed on the old buses was a sign that said 'Go anywhere for 1/–'.
2 We also noticed the adverts on the buses, nowadays buses advertise activities that are going on but these buses advertised items like e.g. baked beans, Macleans toothpaste, shoe polish etc.

Our visit to the London Transport Museum

Sandra and Deborah (14)
On 23rd of Januray we visited the London Transport Museum, we caught a Green Line Bus 715 at the Cross which took us to Hammersmith. We brought four Cheap Day Return Tickets which cost us £2.40 – 60p each. This Green Line bus was very comfortable was more like a coach and had no upper deck. It took us about four hours to get to Hammersmith and was a very enjoyable ride, as the Green Line buses do not stop so frequently often. Arriving at Hammersmith we caught a 267 a red bus to Syon Park which took us about 35 min and cost us 10p each total 40p. We then made our way to the museum. After having our lunch, we look around the Museum. The museum had 26 buses trams, and trains with 2 bus stops. These buses were not the same as the buses on the roads today. Many had no tops they were open buses like you see in old films. Unlike the fares today you could go any distance for 1 shilling. The buses were a lot smaller and seated about 22. Something for you to find out How many people does a 217 bus seat? And How many does a 242 bus seat? Do you know when the single decked buses were first on the roads?

On the buses the seats were like planks of wood with cushions on the top, they didn't look as comfortable. You may not think that bus seats today are comfortable but compare with the older type seats you would!! They often put far to many passenger in the buses and it was often very crampted.

Assessment and criticism

Marking and criticism of children's work is a very vexed question. The knowledge that their work will be assessed is a major factor in the children's sense of the teacher as the chief audience for their writing, and 'marking' is a large part of every teacher's work. It is also *seen* to be so by teachers, their pupils, and the public in general. In fact, so strong is this institutional view, that it is difficult for individual teachers to make changes in their procedures if they wish to. Yet, the Project has a good deal of evidence of the striking changes that can happen in what and how children write when there is no assessment involved, coupled sometimes with the writing being self-chosen. We have quoted some of these elsewhere in this book. Examples are 'Dennis's personal log book' (p.82), 'Why I write what I write' (p. 126), 'Today we did some experiments . . .' (p.146).

Part of the pressure on teachers to correct their students' work in detail and to award marks – and on students to expect this – undoubtedly comes from the examination system, but it does not only come from this. Part of it comes from the largely implicit view of the teacher's role referred to above which is held by nearly everyone. The notion of the teacher as examiner is learned very early, long before the examination system is within sight, though we do not suggest that it is always announced as early as it was for the boy whose writing we quote below:

A mother told us she had asked her six year old son why he didn't write longer stories for his teacher when he wrote such good stories for her. He had replied, 'I don't like writing stories at school. I'm frightened of getting mistakes. I don't know how to spell some words and I forget full stops.'

Here are two of the many short pieces he wrote at school. They are all about the same length.

I like the rocks. In the water there are fish. I catch them. I have got a fish now.

I have a draw. I have a treasure. It is in my cupboard. I take it out sometimes.

We note the short sentences and absence of any connections – which could raise the problem of punctuation. Clearly a high risk situation which he meets by writing as little as possible. In contrast we quote one of the stories he wrote at home for his mother.

The bird that flew across the sea   Anthony (6)
One day I saw a bird. I chast it. It flew over the sea. I wached it. It flew fast and dropped some fethers and then flew away again. I stac at it. I got in a little canoe and I started to row. I folode it everywhere. I would not lose it. I went so fast the boat nearly tipped but i didn't because I pulled the orws to fast I saw a big ship. I got in it. I asked the Kapten to go faster and faster so he did. I cept waching it. I would not take my eyes off it. The bird flew on. The ship went so fast the people were scad so I said to the Kapten go faster and faster. The people got scader and scader. I was not scad. I said to the people do not be scad. I lost the bird.

We note here the length of the story, the wider range of words, the much greater complexity of syntax – 'The ship went so fast the people were scad so I said to the Kapten go faster and faster', and above all the drama of the story, with its climax 'I lost the bird'. In the freedom and security of a nonassessing audience he can draw fully on his resources of language which his school pieces barely hint at.

Assessment in some form is a built-in part of any learning situation and everyone recognises this. The problem as it affects children's learning is linked with their use of their own language and how they see their teacher (and themselves) – matters which we have had to deal with separately in this chapter but which are all part of the complex of factors already referred to and illustrated. We asked ourselves, and some of the teachers we worked with, 'When is a teacher's criticism or advice helpful? Need assessment be as inhibiting as many students find it? Does our analysis of the circumstances of school writing provide us with any general answers to the problem?' We return to this topic in the last section of this chapter in the context of cooperative learning, but it is appropriate here to suggest that for criticism and assessment to be productive a balance needs to be maintained between a number of contrary pressures and that the dynamic of writing probably lies in the tension between these pressures.

In the first place, there is the writer's struggle to say what he wants to say – to satisfy himself – counterbalanced by the need to satisfy his audience. We suggest that in many school situations the balance swings too far in the direction of the audience (the teacher) so that the writer loses, or denies, his sense of what he wants to say. Ian's comments (p.131) are a clear example of this imbalance.

Second, there is the intellectual struggle that a writer has between the facts of his experience or knowledge – one could call it 'getting it right' – and the verbal construction he is making of it in his writing – how he organises it or shapes it. This is particularly difficult in transactional writing, which may be why so many teachers do it for their pupils by means of titles, headings and dictated notes.

More generally, there is the fact that part of growing up is the need to gain recognition from adults of the value of one's own opinions, interests and wishes. The struggle for these 'rights' goes on at home and at school and a fair balance here should mean a more useful role for the teacher's assessment.

The pressures on the teacher reading his students' work are different. Much of what he reads is some sort of reflection of what he has tried to teach so in his case the tension is between how much of this specific learning seems to have occurred and what other values he can see in the work. Moreover, since he has the work of a whole class to read he is almost inevitably influenced by competitive elements. Many teachers struggle to maintain a balance here between their assessment of an individual's progress and their sense of where he should be in comparison with others of his age in the school. We found illuminating what an American teacher, Barbara Zussman, wrote as the result of an enquiry she conducted into how some of the students in a number of schools regarded the teachers' assessment of their work. We quote from her article 'Just a tick is hopeless':

It was apparent from some of the responses that the boys wanted the marking system to be a continuation of the teaching process so that they could improve in the future.
Nicholas (fourth year) wrote:

I think that when some work is going to be marked I don't think the teacher should mark it by her or his self. But it should be marked by the teacher and the pupil. After they have talked about it and by doing this I think it can help the teacher and the pupil.

Julie (fifth year) wrote:

The best way for teachers to work would be firstly to give some sort of mark. Then instead of just writing at the bottom questions that should have been answered in the essay add the points themselves for obviously if I had known the answers I would have put them in.

Barbara Zussman concludes:

Obviously, I was working with a very small sample, but I feel that I gained enough information to see that students are asking to be treated as individuals whose groping attempts to meet our requirements are worthy of consideration and respect. I think they are saying, 'take the time to explain to us what we are doing or not doing to come up to your standards and we'll try. Otherwise you are just turning us off!'

The role of everyday language in learning: some of the problems
Our belief in the importance of personal, everyday language in

learning will be clear from the many illustrations and comments recurring all through this book. Since this is not a local prejudice in favour of one kind of language rather than another, we attempt here to pull these scattered utterances together in a more coherent form. Our view arises from changing notions about the objectivity of knowledge. We think that knowledge is personal: each of us has to remain at the centre of his own learning, and we establish this position chiefly by means of our own language. If this is so, then children's own language, whatever it may be, needs to be not only accepted but also encouraged as a crucial part of their learning.

This ought not to cause problems, but it does because it conflicts sharply with the widespread belief that Standard English is the only 'proper' English and is therefore the language of education. It has been generally taken for granted that the gap between children's everyday language and Standard English should be closed by having children acquire as soon as possible this 'language of education'. Thus the value of children's own everyday language and the importance of their acquiring Standard English are in head-on confrontation.

The problem has two aspects, one educational and one social-political. First, the educational aspect. Behind the debate about everyday language versus other kinds lies the central paradox of language itself. Language faces two ways: outwards and inwards. Its outward face spans the generations and holds relatively constant the *common* forms and *common* meanings developed by speakers of English everywhere in their various communities and groups. Its inward face is towards every man's individual experience which never exactly coincides with anyone else's. So each of us has to use the common (or public) forms of language (sounds, words and sentence patterns) to express the *unique meanings* of our individual experience. To take a simple example, a tiger is a tiger to everyone but everyone's tiger is slightly different because the meanings they attach to the word are different. Again, the things we choose to put into words, and the words which come to hand to express these meanings reflect our unique interpretations of experience. In this sense every utterance we make is new.

This opposition between common forms and individual utterances is the dynamic by which we advance in our use of our mother tongue. We are pushed and pulled both towards the outward 'models' we encounter, and towards the new mintings which reflect our individual meanings and our life histories. The successful resolution of these oppositions is an individual 'voice' which can confidently share its meanings with others (see some of the instances quoted in the first section of this chapter) and is able to move towards a more public voice or a more individual voice according to the demands of different purposes or people. Both directions are necessarily part of one's education – in school and out – but in school they tend to be seen as polarisations instead of contraries which nourish each other, and we have found the weight of school influence put behind the public voice, whereas we would put it behind the individual voice.

In general we would say about everyday *speech* that it is local, comfortable and above all ready-to-hand. Because it is ready-to-hand it is particularly suitable, we would say necessary, for exploratory learning situations and for first drafts of new thinking, and there are many instances in this book of children using their own language in the drafting-thinking process both in speech and in writing. We have found an increasing willingness among teachers to accept children's own spoken language. Changes in classroom situations as we have illustrated in chapter two have created a climate in which real talk (as distinct from teacher-directed question and answer) is commoner in secondary schools than it used to be, and in real talk the struggle with ideas is so obviously a major focus of attention that there is some acceptance of students' own language if only by force of circumstance.

The real trouble comes with the written language. The Bullock Committee commented that they found a scarcity of expressive writing which would represent the written form of the personal everyday speech which they regarded as so important in the first stages of any new learning. They hoped that more opportunity might be given to children to use their own language to express their own views. Peter Medway (project officer for two years) took this argument a stage further in some notes for a lecture. He wrote:

In expressive writing the thinking in the writing is the thinking by which a child gets into a relationship with the topic. Such writing is actually very important because the child is *generating* his commitment as he writes, getting himself to take off point – which many never reach – and also incidentally often working 'internally' at the topic as well.

We think the following writing (taken from *Writing in Science*) by a first year girl about her science lessons illustrates these points. After some straightforward reports had been written the children were invited – but not instructed – to give in any other writing they wanted to. Their teacher encourages a wide range of writing about science. Anna wrote:

Today we did some experiments following on with last weeks. There were some good ones this week. One was Iodine. There was only a tiny bit of it in the test tube. When it was heated it made a deep mauve vapour up the tube with a glitter on the sides of the test tube. When it was cool the deep mauve vapour disappears and only the glitter was left. Another good one was Ammonium Dochromate. It started off as orange granules. But when heated it sparked, bubbled and began to blow out of the tube. The powder began to turn a greeny black powder. When it was cool it stayed a greeny black powder. I think the best one today was lead metal. . . . There were some other things that we done today but they were not as good.

The formal write-up of her various experiments did not satisfy Anna completely. She seems to want to write about her work in chemistry from the centre of her own learning which includes evaluative comments and descriptions in her own language – generating her commitment perhaps.

It is in written language that the social-political aspect of the confusion about Standard English is most damaging. Standard English is in origin a regional dialect of the south-east of England. Because of the power and influence of this region it became a prestigious class dialect and in a still divided society it carries social meanings and influence which other dialects do not. More than this it has come almost universally to be regarded as 'correct' and other forms 'incorrect'. If children are to continue to be the active and independent learners which most of them are when they first go to school we, teachers *and* parents, must begin by accepting their dialect whatever it may be – in speaking and in writing. Yet there is a widespread view among parents and teachers that all 'errors' in writing should be corrected. Let us look at the task of writing from this point of view. First, there is the writer's personal everyday language which may conflict with his teacher's sense of the appropriate language for written school work – it may seem too near speech, yet speech can be nearer to thinking than writing. Anna wrote: 'There was only a tiny bit of it in the test tube.' 'Small quantity' might have been more conventionally acceptable in a science report. We don't know why. Children's writing is full of speech elements like this. Sometimes they have to be corrected and children have, in addition, to cope with the content in their writing, to remember not to use their ready-to-hand language about it, to use someone else's language. Second, there are the dialectal features of their language which conflict with Standard English. Anna wrote: 'There were some other things that we done today but they were not as good.' This is a more difficult issue. The grammar of Standard English is generally accepted in transactional writing for a public audience. Anna was not writing for a public audience and her teacher accepted her dialect form. We suggest that as children gain more experience of a wide range of writing they will learn (or can be taught) the forms appropriate for a public audience. Third, there are all the problems of typography – spelling, punctuation, titles, margins etc. These are conventions to aid the reader and readers need to be reckoned with, though more on some occasions than on others, but these conventions are nothing to do with the formulating-thinking process that writing is.

We suggest that the proofreading treatment of correcting all errors in all that children write is destructive, though no one is to blame. Parents and teachers in putting a major stress on accuracy at all costs are only passing on the expectations set up in them by their own educations. It is part of the aims of a book like this to help to broaden their expectations. We have found a widespread underground resistance movement among school students against these kinds of pressures, and we have quoted some of their views in chapter one and in the earlier part of this chapter. Julie (aged thirteen) seems to sum it up in her assertion of the student's essential independence as a learner: 'They can teach us to spell and punctuate but they can't teach us to imagine, write down what we think, can't drum things into us because we've got our own thoughts.'

We conclude this section with part of the transcript we mentioned in chapter two of a conversation between a teacher in a Yorkshire school and some of his lower-sixth form students. In this discussion the students reveal their sudden awareness of what the spoken language is like and how it differs from the written language, and why. They discuss, in fact, many of the issues raised in this section. This awareness comes through the mutual exploration of the issues and not by the teacher correcting work the students had done.

The teacher had presented his students with copies of a transcript of a previous discussion he had had with them, i.e. he gave them a written down version of their spoken conversation to *read*. It was a shock to them (as it is to most people the first time they read actual speech) and after the first bewilderment had worn off it was a powerful stimulus for discussion about language. What follows is part of that discussion.

Teacher: Er, what is the main difference between the writing that you've got here, which is the writing of your speech – what's the difference between that and normal English that you'd write in your folders?

Joan: 's not English.

Teacher: Which isn't English?

Joan: (laughs)

Teacher: This (pointing at the transcript) isn't English? I think I know what you mean – what do you mean?

Wanda: (Almost inaudibly) It don't read, don't read how you'd pronounce it anyway.

Teacher: It hasn't got the dialect and things like that in, has it? But what do you mean, Joan, by 'It's not English'?

Joan: Well, you wouldn't (indecipherable) English.

Teacher: You wouldn't write like this?

Joan: No.

Teacher: Why? What would you write? What's the difference?

Joan: It's – the grammar isn't right.

Teacher: Can you – yeah think about it; is there anything ungrammatical here? (four seconds pause) I think there is one thing that's ungrammatical that I spotted, that's all. See if you can find – more! (three seconds pause) When Wanda says in the middle of the first page, 'Because if you put us in there we'd know it *were* on', when in fact you'd say 'it wor*', wouldn't you – that's the only ungrammatical bit that's in there. Unless you can prove me wrong. (Chuckle) So it's not the grammar exactly (twenty-four seconds pause) I think I'm going to leave you with that problem. If anyone can decide –

(*'Wor' – a Yorkshire spoken version of 'was')

Beverley: When – this is like we, really, are, i'n't it? (Undertone) 's, um, hard to explain really. This is us what's on this tape, but it's *not* when we write, you know, we . . .

Teacher: Ah.

Beverley: . . . we, we're picking ourselves out all the time when we write, but this is how we are normally.

Teacher: Ah yeah, I know what you mean; that's I think what, what Joan meant in a way. Joan was describing the language, but you're describing the person, but you're making the same point I think.

Beverley: Yeah.

Teacher: (Slowly) So this is you, the way you are –

Beverley: Yeah.

Teacher: But writing, isn't quite you. And you said because you're always picking yourselves out; now what, what exactly is that?

Beverley: Well, I mean – er, you know, we wouldn't put 'thee', 'thou', 'that', down on paper would we?

Teacher: No.

Beverley: (Slowly, thoughtfully) We, make, we'd, we wouldn't write that down, we'd have to find another form of –

Teacher: Yeah.

Beverley: More or less.

Teacher: Yeah.

Beverley: This is what I mean.

Denise: Well, it's like when Wanda says . . .

Beverley: It's down on paper.

Denise: . . . We wouldn't dare say 'owt', we wouldn't write . . .

Teacher: Oh no.

Denise: . . . 'owt', I mean we wouldn't write that down on – when we're writing properly.

Teacher: You mean you'd have to say, 'We wouldn't say anything', wouldn't you, you'd have to write it like that. That's dialect really, or accent. (Very slowly) So do you think that you find writing more difficult than speaking? (three seconds pause)

Beverley: Yeah.

Teacher: Is it?

Susan: Yeah. (Laughter)

Joan: She spoke! (Less laughter)

Teacher: Right. (Slowly) Because you have to make an effort to put your thoughts into a certain *form* when you're writing.

Girls: (Quietly) Yeah.

Wanda: (Quietly) You don't have to make an effort.

Teacher: *You* don't have to make an effort?

Wanda: (Very quietly) No.

Teacher: It just comes naturally. But you're still changing yourself; is that – do you agree with Beverley on this? I mean, I don't know . . .

Girl: Yeah.

Beverley: Well you are 'cos you can't write (indecipherable) English.

Wanda: Everybody speaks different to what they write.

Teacher: Yeah, we're trying – Beverley's trying to *explain why*, and she says it's because when you're talking you just are yourself, but when you're writing you've got to, kind of put it in a certain form.

Wanda: You're still yourself when you're writing – everybody has a different style of writing, don't they? I mean it's, it i'nt any harder to write than it is to speak – you, you still –

Joan: Aye, but if you write down how you –

Denise: (Slowly) I couldn't write down how I talk, I mean –

Joan: You can't, can you?

Denise: If I talk like this I couldn't write that down, I'd write it down sort o'proper English.

Teacher: (Quietly) Mm. Well, that's kind of what Wanda's saying, you know, that it comes natural in fact, that you don't have to make any grinding effort –

Wanda: No, there's no difference . . .

Susan: Ah.

Wanda: . . . between speaking and writing 'cos you're only using vocabulary, aren't yer?

Susan: Well – but you've *learnt* 'ow to do it, when you were little y–, you, you probably spelt cat with a 'k' or summat like that, wouldn't yer, because –

Teacher: Ah, that's a very good point I think; that, er, you weren't aware of learning how to speak, you just learnt how to speak.

Joan: You speak like you hear other people though.

Teacher: Ah yeah. Do you *write* like you *read* other people?

Wanda ⎫ No, you write your own.
  Girl ⎭ Everybody, everybody writes their own.

Teacher: They have their own style of writing. Mmm. (three seconds pause) But Wanda, you just said there's no difference between writing and speech (short mumble, from Wanda?) But there *is*. (Laughter)

Susan: A lot! (Giggles. Five seconds pause)

Joan: It's all t'same, it's just that, that's your *kind* o' talking.

Girls: Mmm – er – (Pause. It sounds on the tape as though someone was saying, 'It's quiet'.)

Wanda: Everybody's different, there's no differ–, there's no difference in what I write an' what I speak, only pronunciation (short mumble), really. (Very quietly) Only I write correct, I write, I write it proper when I write it down; I don't speak it proper – everybody talks different to what they write, don't they?

Teacher: (Quietly) Ar right, so –

Joan: Back where you start? (Laughing)

We think this transcript and the situation it arose from illustrate both a teacher-student relationship based on cooperation rather than authority, and an acceptance of the students' language.

Tracking the development of good transactional writing: some of the problems

Since the bulk of school knowledge is transmitted through the written language in its transactional forms, reading books and writing attract increasing attention as students go up the secondary school; and most students find both difficult. In the fourth and fifth years the pressure of anxiety mounts for both students and teachers, and on the whole results in the kind of 'knowledge' presented in the kind of writing quoted in the beginning of chapter three. We were interested in tracking, at all stages in the secondary school, the circumstances in which students make their own sense out of new information, restructure it to fit into their expanding world picture and 'remain at the centre of their own learning'. Some of our findings are reported and commented on in chapter three; there almost all examples of writing come from the eleven to thirteen age group. Here we indicate where our enquiry has led us in the particular circumstances of the fourth and fifth years.

We had two specific quests. First, 'book knowledge', because of the importance given to it in schools. We wanted to track the circumstances in which students were able to make their own sense of this kind of secondary experience. Second, the problem of the 'isolated examples' of good transactional writing. Could we find circumstances in which there was enough good writing in a single class, or group, for us to be able to generalise the conditions? This last has been a general aim and we think that what we have to say about the conditions for good transactional writing may in fact have a wider significance.

Most of the good transactional writing we found in the work of older (as well as younger) students started from first-hand experience. The examples we quote here come from two groups (or classes) in the same school. The students were in their fifth year, and the writing comes from the folders of ongoing work they were collecting to present for o level (Mode III) social studies or CSE (Mode III) community studies. We have commented elsewhere in this book on the limiting effects of examinations on learning and writing, and have been making some case studies of written work from schools where Mode III-type examinations (assessment of course work) are taken. It is, of course, quite possible for folders of course work to be composed of set work marked in the usual way, so it is not the type of examination *per se* which causes changes. It is rather that, given a favourable environment for learning, then the writing that arises from it is the matter that is assessed for the examination. So this type of examination *permits* the kind of work normally done in the school to continue.

The first-hand experience in these course-work studies was extended, as one would hope, by secondary experience of different kinds. Different students made different use of secondary sources, some going chiefly to books for their information, others relying on what they learned from other people. Most of them draw on books and teachers for the way they organise and present their work, and in addition, they reflect on the study they have been engaged in and assess its value to them, and in doing so demonstrate some kind of perspective for their learning. At this point, therefore, we want to suggest that one of the conditions for good transactional writing is where circumstances encourage the *interplay of first-hand and secondary experience*, and that a further condition is that there should be opportunities for the students to encounter good and varied *'models' of transactional language*.

The term 'model' here needs a word of explanation. It is not used to refer to an exemplar that is deliberately imitated. It means here the sense of what something is like, arrived at by repeated encounters. Language is learned by meeting it and using it. In chapter one we discussed how experience of living teaches us to recognise the kind of discourse that we are encountering. For instance, we seldom fail to recognise instructions when we meet them. Again we can usually identify a sales talk, even disguised as a story, or a sermon, though children can be deceived here because they are, as yet, in the process of learning the functions of these different kinds of discourse. In this sense all the examples of language use which we encounter in our daily life are 'models'.

We found in many schools considerable poverty of varied 'models' of transactional writing. Up to the fifth year students tended to work from a single textbook, supplemented by their teachers' notes. They just did not have enough experience of good and varied language in their different subjects.

We begin with two o level projects in social studies. The first, by a fifth form girl, is a very extensive project called 'The development of New Walk, Leicester'. All we have space for here are quotations from her introduction and from the first half of her conclusion, but we think they indicate her purpose and the scope of her study, show something of her sources, and reveal something of the interaction between her first-hand knowledge of Leicester and the very large extent to which she has drawn on secondary sources of information. The quality of her writing reflects a wide experience of 'models' of the written language.

The development of New Walk   Janet (15)
Introduction (extract)
I chose New Walk for my project because I feel it is an important part of Leicester's heritage which should be preserved. Its attractiveness led me to investigate into its past history. It fascinates me to see the old houses which stand, majestically defying the march of progress.

Another reason for my choice of project was that I wanted to learn some history without my head being crammed with dates of wars and revolutions. I learned how New Walk developed and about the life of a family who lived there. That is real history, the history of life, people and places around you which otherwise would pass by unnoticed.

I intend to research into the history of New Walk, the plans for its redevelopment, a case history of a house in New Walk, and the reasons why the Walk should be preserved.

This shows her as confident in her role as a student, independent in her view of history, and she can use the language of books as her own. The two paragraphs from her conclusion which follow reveal a good deal of reading about problems of conservation, planning and development, and local information, as well as first-hand knowledge of the city. She is at ease with general ideas, and explores as well as reports problems:

After doing the project I am not so sure that this is quite what is meant by conservation. A city has been accepted as the place for work, not as a residential community, though there is a suggestion for a residential complex between High Street and Silver Street. The Council have asked for public opinion on the matter and issued two information sheets. The area is full of little quaint old shops. With rents being lower than anywhere else in the city centre, one-man businesses are able to operate to make a profit. These would all be lost in any large-scale redevelopment.

We hope our city thrives on business and because of this you get a conservation of a city centre which 'dies' between 6 and 9 pm and 2 and 8 am. Our cities are like giant factories set in motion by the arrival of their workers and closed by their exit. In our expanding society land is becoming in very short supply. If our cities are not renovated for habitation now, we are limiting space for the people of the next generation to live. Without the conservation of places like New Walk, we are destroying the city's character to make way for prefabricated concrete office blocks that have a nine-to-five halflife.

We took Janet's study as our first example because it is so clearly the kind of work people expect in fifth form students; it is a bookish study in content and language (which is not to decry it at all) and it is very different from the passage about Josiah Wedgwood's innovations in industry (quoted on p.64) which reveals no such engagement with the topic as this study does.

Our second example from this fifth year o level group of students is by a boy. It stems from a situation in his own experience, and in one sense it is a narrative, but as his introduction shows he extends it into general questions which go beyond his own family.

Social studies project on the rehousing of my grandparents
Brian (15)

Introduction
This project is about the rehousing of my mother's parents,

Mr and Mrs J. Bird. They now live in a new set of flats, but before, they lived for thirty-five years in an old town-type house. The project will be about their views towards moving. The change of friends and community. Will it affect their way of life? Benefits of the new flat – heating etc. Criticism of the old house.

Besides answering these questions I will also try to find out how the Council go about the rehousing of individuals. How do they approach people?

Then follows a narrative summary of the events in his grandparents' lives in relation to their house. We quote the last four paragraphs to illustrate the quality of his reporting and writing.

. . . this was very sad for my grandma and grandad knowing that they had to move from their own house after having bought it. I am sure they thought that it would last them the rest of their lives.

Gradually since 1972, people were leaving Vann Street, some moving into flats in Leicester and some moving outside Leicestershire altogether.

Housing Inspectors called on grandma and grandad asking them where they wanted to go. Alternative houses were offered all around Leicester, but grandma and grandad were not sure where they wanted to go.

Nearing the present day they mentioned that they were hopeful of moving into some new flats that were being built just around the corner.

Everything climaxed.

He then constructed a questionnaire for his grandparents, and this and the answers ('all answered by my grandma') are the next two items in his folder. We print the questionnaire and two of the answers.

Questionnaire for my grandparents

1 How do you feel about losing the old house and gaining a new one?
2 What benefits of a new house can you foresee?
3 How do you feel to see your old neighbourhood disappearing and a change of friends, neighbourhood and community?
4 How were you approached by the Council?
5 How was the 'disturbance' money given out?
6 How are the flats designed?

Sample answers written by his grandmother:

1 It was very sad to know that we had got to move after buying it and having it for thirty-five years. Grandad will miss his garden at the back.
5 People who have been living in the houses for five years qualify for the 'disturbance money'. If you have been living in the house for five years the 'disturbance money' is three times the rateable value plus twenty-five pounds for removal of furniture, cookers etc. On top of this we also got the price for the house which is £3,100.

We shall not receive this 'upheaval money' until we move into our new flat.

On the Compulsory Purchase Order of 15th September 1972, the area was classed as unfit for human habitation. Through our estate agent we objected that we didn't live in dirt and grit. We found out that when the area was classed as unfit for human habitation it meant that not each individual house was unfit for human habitation (like ours) but that the area as a whole was classed unfit for human habitation. Later we were changed off para (a) to para (b) of the Compulsory Purchase Order thus receiving more money.

The longest item in his folder is his account of the move called 'The big day'. It is a lively, detailed account with vignettes of uncles and aunts and cousins who helped with the move. The family is presented, dialogue and all. His last item is a photograph from the *Leicester Mercury* with the following caption – 'Derelict homes waiting for the demolition men to move in. A distressing sight for the families who used to live in them.' Alongside this picture of ruinous houses he has written:

> After having read this my grandma nearly bit my head off for writing this piece with the photo. I told her I had took it from the *Mercury*. She answered saying that this photo was taken down one of the oldest streets and these are the worst condition of all the houses. She no doubt thought that I was implying that her house looked like this.

Then he adds in brackets, as though his grandma's reaction had made him think again about the human implications of the photograph and the caption:

> (Although they don't say 'a typical view' in the quote, they are on the border to saying this.)

We have quoted a good deal from this study for several reasons. It is very different from Janet's study which seems to us in the best academic tradition, yet this one also is involved, independent and thoughtful work. But while we can see in both studies the dynamic interaction of first-hand experience and information from secondary sources, this study draws primarily on the face-to-face experience of other people, though in its organisation – the introduction, the questionnaire, the arrangement of the items – we can see the influence of books. Brian has also involved his family in his study, not only as sources of information but as active contributors, and what a model his grandma's writing is – in our view, an admirable example of what good transactional writing should be like. His own writing draws on all his resources of speech, but it has its more formal features too in the questionnaire and in other items which we have not the space to include.

The next examples we report or quote from come from the fifth year CSE group working on community studies.

This course involves the students in spending some time actually working with various groups or individuals. They keep diaries and much of the work in their folders is based on these. Angela worked for a year with a group of physically-handicapped people who came into the college one afternoon a week. Her study records her starting uncertainties and fears, the events that took place and how her experiences deeply altered the way she views handicapped people. It is essentially a record of her growth of self-knowledge as a result of her work with handicapped people, and of her growing capacity to understand other people. It does not apparently draw on any book knowledge. It is written in her own everyday language with many quoted conversations, and in her conclusions she reflects on what she has learned from these people. Her teacher wrote at the end of this study, 'I feel I have learned a lot with you, Angela.'

Without in any way belittling the traditional sources of information we feel it is salutory to read a study where learning is so manifestly happening without the benefit of books.

Lynn worked one day a week for a year in a playschool. She wrote:

I have really enjoyed doing this project and I would like to go into it further when I have some more time. I have learnt a great deal by being with young children. . . . Before I went to playschool I had always wanted to work with children but I hadn't any experience. Now I feel more confident with young children. When I'm in the sixth form I will keep going to the playgroup as when I leave school I want to take the JNEB course, and I need as much experience with children as I can get. I also feel I will remember a lot of these when I have children of my own.

The last example we have space for in this section comes from Debra whose study was on 'The problems of adopting a coloured baby'. Like Brian she drew the adopting parents into her study.

She too sent them a questionnaire and the mother replied very fully to the questions. In her conclusion Debra wrote:

This project has been very interesting. I only wish that more time was allowed as I have only been able to briefly touch each stage of adoption.

When I first started my project I was very ignorant towards the adoption practice, I certainly did not realise that so many people were involved with the placing of one child. Some times I found it hard to think of the child as any other ordinary, fun-loving. child. I tryed hard to put myself in the shoes of the child, the natural parents and the adoptive parents. This was hard to do as you tend to think of them as some kind of machines.

I think there are still a few aspects of the adoption procedure that could be improved upon. . . .

I would like to see a project written by a child who is adopted. I think that the problems would be understood much better. The opinions of the child would be really interesting to read.

Her teacher commented, 'A good point – it would make interesting reading – but yours has too.'

In tackling this topic Debra had perforce to come to grips with a good deal of detailed legal and procedural information, but throughout she keeps her grip on what to her seems the central issue – what does it feel like to be an adopted child, or to be the parent of one? She seems aware that too strong a focus on procedures can be dehumanising.

The outstanding feature of these studies (and of others in the group which we have not been able to quote) is that they are genuine communications of experience of learning. They relate to the writers' own lives and interests and reflect a sense of being on the threshold of the adult world. In this they are realistic educational documents, and they contrast violently both in content and language with most traditional examination answers. We would however repeat the point made earlier: the different type of examination does not cause the change; it allows it to happen when many other conditions in the context of learning are present.

We have dealt with this question of the development of transactional writing in the upper school at considerable length because it is the main kind of language used in school across the curriculum. It is also the language which most troubles students – and their teachers. We have tried to show that our evidence suggests that the way into it is not by recipe but by the constant interaction of a personal viewpoint with information from varied secondary sources. We think this dynamic is the actual process of learning as well as of language growth.

At the beginning of this chapter we discussed the problem of 'isolated' examples of writing that showed commitment, and suggested that for such commitment to happen on a wider scale whole environments for learning would need to be changed. All the writing we have quoted in this section came from the same school but not from the same class. So these writings are not isolated examples, and we think therefore we can make the general point that for changes to go beyond the occasional individual student there must be enough teachers who share a view about learning and language to create a different set of possibilities in the school. We suggest that in this school such a different set of possibilities had been created.

Changes in notions of progress in learning and language

From time to time we have arranged small consultative conferences for up to a dozen teachers to discuss with them what seemed to be the growing points in their work and ours. There was no set agenda, only the intention to explore in talk, and possibly write about the outcomes of the talk. We think it is significant that at a conference with the science teachers who produced *Writing in Science*, the question that was returned to again and again was creative *thinking and creativity* – what we meant by it, whether it was the same thing in all subjects, what learning environments fostered it etc. At a comparable conference with humanities teachers, the central issue that emerged was co-operative learning – between students, and between teachers and students. We discussed changes in the teaching-learning relationship, the implications of self-chosen work, the notion of partnerships in learning, the role of assessment within this, the points in the learning process when a teacher can help without distorting the student's work etc.

We don't think it is entirely accidental that these two particular issues arose so persistently. This is what the findings and hypotheses of the writing research point towards, though it only became apparent as the ideas were realised in the work coming from classrooms. Also, as we said at the beginning of this chapter, educational research only focusses and defines things that are already happening, so we think these issues will have a wider currency than might seem from their location in the work of the Project. We shall, therefore, take 'creativity' and 'co-operative learning' as the starting points for discussing changes in notions of progress in learning and language generally.

Intention is said to be the motivating force for thinking as well as action, so creativity (in a very general sense) would seem to be related to intention. This seems a long way from creative writing, dance-drama and work in the art room which is, perhaps, where many people would locate creativity in school. But it is clearly absurd to believe that creative thinking can be attached in this way to a limited number of activities. We needed to look at creativeness more generally and our 'across the curriculum' brief forced us to do this. In discussing problems of commitment to learning we kept returning to intention and the kind of environments which would permit it and sustain it. Young children are curious and persistent and eager. One could call intention robust at this stage. In the secondary school it is, for whatever reason, a delicate thing. If it exists in relation to school work at all, it is easily snuffed out, or it drifts away, or is superseded by another feeble interest, but since so much of schooling pays such limited attention to children's intentions it is not surprising that creative thinking or creativity don't flourish, or at best survive in those activities that are least susceptible to other people's programming – improvised drama or writing poems for instance.

So the constraints in school on intention and choice needed to be looked at, and it became clear that, however benevolent, teachers' intentions for their pupils are dominant and reach into almost all corners of school life. In the context of learning this raises the question of how a teacher can help a pupil without imposing a structure on his pupil's thinking (and work) which hinders rather than helps the pupil's development. There is a delicate balance needed here which changes with different phases of the student's commitment to his project. Moreover, this kind of balance depends on a teaching-learning relationship which is not one of authority. The analysis made by Peter Medway and Ivor Goodson of the kind of help a teacher might give in these different phases and of the relationship it depends on is illuminating:

Cooperation is not a euphemism, a gentler way of doing the same old thing, only by persuasion rather than imposition. The implied equality is meant to be taken seriously. The learning relationship, starting on the teacher's side with a commitment to reciprocity, progresses (when all goes well) to the point where it is experienced as a reality.

A cooperative learning experience that reaches the crucial learning threshold might pass through three stages. After 'browsing' in the 'environment' the student eventually says 'I want to do something on the Second World War.' He gets the reply 'OK. Get started. Here's some books and magazines, there's a filmstrip you can look at.'

Then follows a period during which the teacher can feel quite anxious about what's going on. There may be a lot of copying out of books, drawing pictures, unrelated bits and pieces of knowledge being collected – useless knowledge it may seem, and so it may be. But what may be going on is a process of exploration in which the student, often unconsciously, feels around the topic to locate the real source of its attraction for him – some difficulty or worry or preoccupation or powerful feeling relating to it.

The teacher watches all this and tries to detect underlying themes and concerns in the student's busy activity. At the same time he tries to gently maintain it and restrain himself from criticism. By now the student is beginning to get clearer about what it is in the topic that really interests him and tries to bring it into focus. 'So what you're really on about is the casual pointless way people could get killed, in ways that couldn't make any sense to them. You live your whole life, have an education, a family, fillings in your teeth, and end up in a ditch after some minor skirmish with an unimportant enemy outpost that was going to withdraw one minute later anyway.' The teacher goes on to suggest further ways of exploring this central interest.

The student is now experiencing the satisfaction of successfully getting into the topic for himself and bringing it under control. He's developed tenacity and perseverance, makes statements he can back up, suggests hypotheses with confidence, and can improvise from knowledge.

The project is out of the intensive care unit and can be subjected to rough handling – the teacher can speak his mind without fear of killing it stone dead or putting the student down. The relationship has become robust and stimulating to both sides. The student is interested in the teacher's opinion of his work, enjoys his company and challenges him; the teacher has got interested in the student and the topic (about which he now knows a lot more than he did). Both now feel the mutuality which started off as an abstract ideal.

We think this hypothetical situation, based on experience of working in this way, illustrates a learning environment which supports the growth of creative thinking; and it hinges on the teacher's 'commitment to reciprocity' i.e. cooperative learning.

It will be clear by now that we see as creative the process by which we use secondary experience to construct our own interpretation of events, and this brings any work that a student may be doing in any subject within the possible orbit of creativity. Are we stretching the notion too far? We don't think so. We have spoken before about alternative modes of representation – the explicit and the mythic – and we are suggesting that it is erroneous to think that imagination is at work in one and not the other. 'Imagine' is a broad and variously interpreted term. We think it involves envisaging possibilities, imagined or real – Kelly's 'Let us suppose . . .', predicting, connecting, transforming or just 'making'.

The analysis quoted above came from two teachers who think it important for children to make choices from the outset and settle for themselves what it is they want to work at. They think teacher-directed programmes fail for all but a few because they don't match children's interests and intentions or their views about what is important. Other teachers, however, believe that there is a corpus of knowledge to be learnt, and some think the sequencing of this matters. George Goldby, in an article in *Writing in Science* makes clear the nature of this debate as it applies to science education. He writes:

Science as a process: a change in emphasis

There seem to be two different and conflicting goals in science education: one is to teach a body of accepted knowledge, the other is to teach the *process* by which that knowledge has been acquired. One of these two goals – the former – continues to be dominant in science teaching today, but I believe that the latter goal – the process of science – is by far the more important. The way we work is bound up with the way we use language, and a change in emphasis from science as knowledge to science as a process would require, amongst other things, a change in the way we use language in science education.

When science is taught as knowledge, the students are drawn towards a static, predetermined end; but when science is taught as a process, the end is neither fixed nor predictable: it is instead the process of the investigation, and the outcome of this process is essentially uncertain.

The part played by writing in science education reflects the choice of goal. If, in the end, the lesson is directed towards static impersonal knowledge, then transactional informational writing will be the appropriate method of expression and communication. The dominant part that this informational writing still plays in the science work of school children shows how far we avoid the development of scientific skill or method. Science teachers reveal by what they ask the students to write that they see little room for self-expression and exploration in the activity which they provide.

These comments reflect not only some changing views about science education but changing views about knowledge. Contrary to popular belief some writers and teachers are claiming the *subjectivity* of knowledge – the knower can't be separated from the known.

Changes in the way people see knowledge affects how they see learning, and teaching, and the learner. Since everything a teacher does in his role as a teacher has an hypothesis about learning behind it – implicit if not explicit – we can begin to see how far-reaching in their effects are changes in attitude towards knowledge.

We have noted for instance changes in how teachers see themselves in relation to their pupils – partners (senior partners perhaps) rather than authorities, so the word 'teaching' becomes hyphenated, 'teaching-learning', education becomes more of a dialogue. Secondly, the learner may be seen as someone in a state of transition rather than someone who is wrong or stupid (see Corinne's piece, p.102). Thirdly, progress in language may be seen as the ability to use language more widely rather than more 'correctly'. Fourthly, notions of assessment are beginning to be affected by these other changes, but because assessment procedures are so strongly institutionalised and are related to the structure of our society in all its multifarious sorting procedures, they are particularly resistant to change. Finally, people begin to attend to different kinds of problems. What constituted these problems was always there but they weren't seen as problems until other changes gave a shake to the box and the kaleidoscope presented a different pattern. Who, for instance, might have predicted ten years ago that science teachers would concern themselves with creativity? It needs to be said, however, that these changes are part of more general changes in society and should not be seen as isolated within an educational context.

We gloss this analysis by quotations from the work of another student from the o level community studies group. We think his long study illustrates most of the matters we have been discussing in this chapter, though it is impossible to convey its general quality in a few quotations. It is sixty-three pages long – single-space typing with some reproduced illustrations which communicate in a kind of counterpoint. The title page announces him independent, confident but aware of possibilities and commenting on himself as he presents his topics.

Community Studies Project
Thought of, written, and realised by Ian Capewell.

His contents page reads:

He is aware of the danger of losing himself in the reading he has done and is specific about his efforts to present his own account of possible alternative societies in the future. He writes:

. . . What I am putting forward is a number of ideas that are original, to the extent that I thought of them all myself, without stealing, or even mixing any other writer's ideas. (I managed this by reading nothing previously written about the future.) I'm not claiming that I'm completely original in my thoughts (nobody could claim that), only that I came to these following ideas with no outside assistance . . .

This subsection on the brighter prospects of the future is in fact nearly half his study. He takes up most of the contemporary problems such as population growth, living space, food, housing, world peace etc. It would be difficult not to see this work as 'creative'. He explores his topic in detail, he asks questions of himself, and he hypothesises.

We quote part of his 'Foreward' which explains how he 'came about his project', which he unravels in the casual, uncommitted start and the gradual but incidental development of a powerful interest. It is interesting also in that it supports the Medway/ Goodson analysis of the stages by which a learning experience may reach the crucial learning threshold.

I could encounter some trouble in explaining how I came about my project, mainly because I am having trouble myself in remembering what first put me on to it. I can only conclude that it was an accumulation of thoughts and ideas. The first point I can actually point to and say, I knew what I was doing for my project, was near the end of the fourth year. Before that I was doing a project on drugs, but I had no wish to continue it, probably to do with it not being a very original idea, I was interested in drugs, but it never went further than just a curiousity.

I suppose if I want to attribute it to one single line of thought, I could lay it on my satiricalness. In the fourth year I had a rather strong attack of cynicism, which was directed at our society (although I still do have this quality, I tend to think it has either been watered down, or has gone deeper into my subconscious, I have also become less extreme, which 'I think I did to be different' but now I truly believe in my less extreme, but still unusual ideas). It was a short while before a general election, and for the first time I rearly began to take an interest in politics, I came out of the other side disillusioned with British politics. It was probably due to that, that I (out of curiousity) looked up that 'dirty word' communism, the result was a bit supprising, because I couldn't see what some people had against it, in fact I quite liked the idea. I began to take an intrest in Russian affairs, this curiousity for the socialist way of life began to spread within me. I suppose I realised that this is what I was searching for, I like the idea of living in a socialist system, hard or not, I like the idea of living together and sharing comforts and hardships. Not wishing to preach but I had the feeling of finding something of extreme importance to myself, something that before now had been hidden to me.

And so I was set upon the path, I began to take an intrest in the different societies that lived outside (and within) our own. And I am quite proud of the fact that I thought of the project myself, and then offered my ideas to my teacher, who agreed that it should be my project.

Once this had been reached I began to read a number of books on the subject, and got deeply interested in it. I was under way.

Implications

All this suggests to us that changing the learning-writing opportunities means changing many things in the school context in terms of who for and what for. The Bullock Report specifically concerns itself with the relation of language to learning and with language across the curriculum. It suggests that schools should work out language policies to help them in making more consistent and informed efforts to develop language. As a result some schools are beginning to discuss these matters, and these discussions we feel must be valuable. We, however, think actual language policies should be approached with caution. All that we have observed in our work and have presented in this book suggests that no *single* operation will be effective. More than that, if our analysis is correct, then attempts to formulate and put into practice a language policy in a school which does not also take into account the other interconnected changes will only be tinkering with surface features and may actually make learning through language opportunities worse rather than better.

Summary

We have raised in this chapter what seem to us to be the most significant elements in the network of changes we have perceived in our four years' work. They are:

1 How a learner sees himself.
2 A writer's sense of audience.
3 Assessment and criticism.

4 The role of everyday language in learning: some of the problems.
5 Tracking the development of good transactional writing: some of the problems.
6 Changes in notions of progress in learning and language.
7 Implications.

References

GOLDBY, G. (1975) 'Science as a process: a change in emphasis' in *Writing in Science* (Schools Council Writing across the Curriculum Project) Ward Lock Educational

KELLY, G. A. (1969) 'The language of hypothesis' in B. Maher (ed) *Clinical Psychology and Personality: The Selected Papers of George Kelly* New York: John Wiley

LEWIS, R. (1975) 'Language and learning in the primary school' in *English in Education* 9, 2, summer

MEDWAY, P. and GOODSON, I. (1975) *Language and Learning in the Humanities* (Schools Council Writing across the Curriculum Project) Ward Lock Educational

ZUSSMAN, B. (1975) 'Just a tick is hopeless' in *Some Issues from the Bullock Report* (Schools Council Writing across the Curriculum Project) Ward Lock Educational

Bibliography

BARNES, D., BRITTON, J., ROSEN, H. (1969) *Language, the Learner and the School* Penguin (1971 revised edition)

BERGER, P.L. and LUCKMANN, T. (1966) *The Social Construction of Reality* Penguin

BERNSTEIN, B. (1975) *Class, Codes and Control Volume 3: Towards a Theory of Educational Transmissions* Routledge and Kegan Paul

BRITTON, J. (1967) (ed) *Talking and Writing* Methuen

BRITTON, J. (1970) *Language and Learning* Penguin

BRITTON, J. *et al* (1975) *The Development of Writing Abilities (11-18)* (Schools Council Research Studies) Macmillan Education

BURGESS, C. *et al* (1973) *Understanding Children Writing* Penguin

CASHDAN, A. and GRUGEON, E. (1973) (eds) *Language in Education: A Source Book* Routledge and Kegan Paul

DES (1975) *A Language for Life* (Bullock Report) HMSO

D'ARCY, P. (1974) *Reading for Meaning Volume 2 The Reader's Response* (Report of Schools Council survey) Hutchinson

DENNISON, G. (1972) *The Lives of Children* Penguin

DIXON, J. (1974) 'Processes of formulation in group discussion' in *Educational Review* 26

EMIG, J. (1971) *The Composing Processes of Twelfth Graders* Urbana, Illinois: National Council of Teachers ·of English

HALLIDAY, M.A.K. (1973) 'Relevant models of language' in *Explorations in the Functions of Language* Arnold

JONES, A. and MULFORD, J. (1971) (eds) *Children Using Language* Oxford University Press

KELLY, G.A. (1963) *A Theory of Personality* New York: Norton

KELLY, G.A. (1969) 'The language of hypothesis' in B. Maher (ed) *Clinical Psychology and Personality* New York: John Wiley

KUHN, T. (1970 revised edition) *The Structure of Scientific Revolutions* Chicago: University of Chicago Press

LANGER, S.K. (1953) *Feeling and Form* Routledge and Kegan Paul

LEWIS, R. (1975) 'Language and learning in the primary school' in *English in Education* 9, 2, summer

MCCORMICK, K.M. *A Study of Some Aspects of Exploratory Small-Group Talk* Unpublished MA thesis, London University

MARTIN, N. *et al* (1975) *Understanding Children Talking* Penguin

MOFFETT, J. (1968) *Teaching the Universe of Discourse* New York: Houghton Mifflin

OLSON, D.R. and BRUNER, J.S. (1974) 'Learning through experience and learning through media' in D.R. Olson (ed) *Media and Symbols: The Forms of Expression, Communication and Education* (NSSE 73rd Yearbook Part 1) Chicago: University of Chicago Press

POLANYI, M. (1962) *Personal Knowledge* Routledge and Kegan Paul

ROGERS, C.R. (1970) 'Towards a theory of creativity' in P.E. Vernon (ed) *Creativity* Penguin

ROSEN, C. and H. (1973) *The Language of Primary School Children* (Schools Council Project on Language Development in the Primary School) Penguin

VYGOTSKY, L.S. (1962) *Thought and Language* Boston: MIT Press

WEIR, R. (1962) *Language in the Crib* The Hague: Mouton

WRITING ACROSS THE CURRICULUM PROJECT

(1973) *From Information to Understanding*

(1973) *Why Write?*

(1973) *From Talking to Writing*

(1974) *Keeping Options Open*

(1975) *Writing in Science*

(1975) *Language and Learning in the Humanities*

(Ward Lock Educational 1976)

YOUNG, M.F.D. (1971) (ed) *Knowledge and Control* Collier Macmillan

Index

List of students' writing and talk